GHOST ENCOUNTERS

THE LINGERING SPIRITS OF NORTH DEVON

HELEN HOLLICK
WITH **KATHY HOLLICK**

TAW RIVER
PRESS

GHOST ENCOUNTERS: The Lingering Spirits Of North Devon
by Helen Hollick
with Kathy Hollick
includes two bonus short stories

All views and opinions are the authors' own.
© Helen Hollick 2025 © Kathy Hollick 2025
Photographs © Kathy Hollick and © Helen Hollick, or as accredited.

Cover Design © 2025 Cathy Helms Avalon Graphics
Cover Illustration © 2025 Chris Collingwood

The rights of Helen Hollick and Kathy Hollick to be identified as the authors of this work has been asserted by them in accordance with the Copyright, Designs and Patents Acts 1988

All rights reserved. No part of this book may be used or reproduced, stored in a retrieval system, or transmitted in any form, or by any means, electronic, mechanical, photocopying, recording or otherwise without the written permission of the copyright holder except in the case of brief quotation embodied in critical articles and reviews.

ISBN
978-1-0687721-8-4 Paperback
978-1-0687721-9-1 E-Book

Published by Taw River Press
https://www.tawriverpress.co.uk

To all our friends who remain among us because they want to.

CONTENTS

1. Welcome to North Devon
2. What Are Ghosts?
3. Home and Our House Guests
4. Close to Home
5. Out and About
6. Further Afield North Devon - Inland
7. Venturing Onto Exmoor
8. Further Down the Coast
9. Barnstaple
10. Beyond Barnstaple
11. Four-Footed Beasts

- Conclusion
- Extra Encounters -
- A Bonus: Two Short Stories: *The Old House. The Bridge*
- Acknowledgements
- Before You Go
- Further Reading

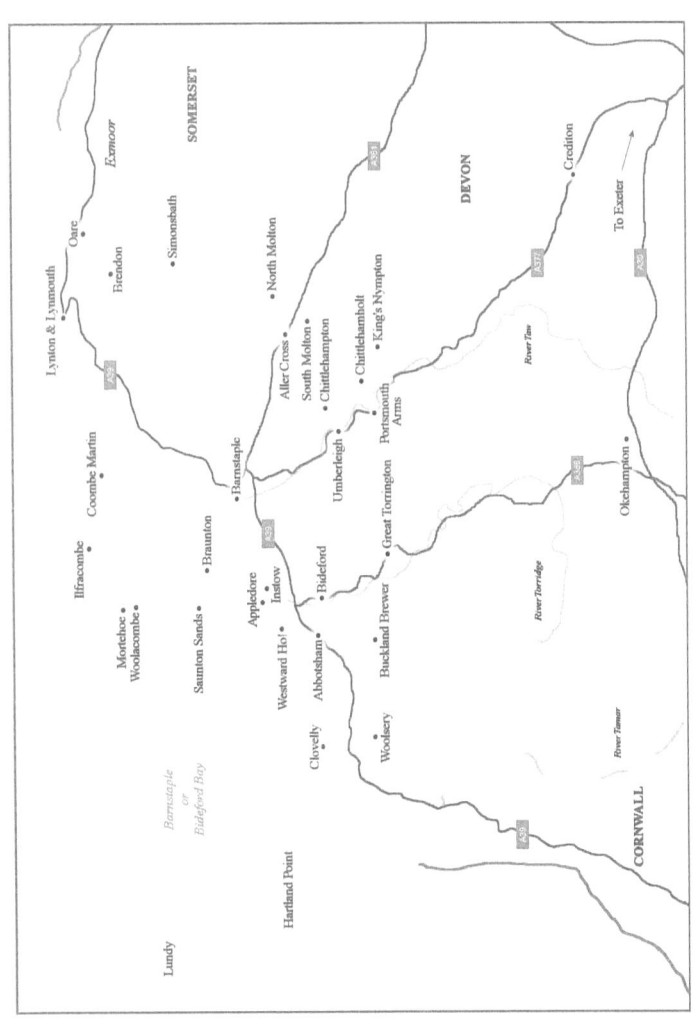

North Devon © M.L.P.

ABOUT HELEN HOLLICK

Known for her captivating storytelling and rich attention to historical detail, Helen might not see ghosts herself, but her nautical adventure series, and some of her short stories, skilfully blend the past with the supernatural, inviting readers to step into worlds where the boundaries between the living and the dead blur.

Her historical fiction spans a variety of periods, with a particular focus on the Dark Ages and the early medieval period. Works like *The Pendragon's Banner* series offer vivid portrayals of both historical events and the fantastical elements that shape them. Her gift lies in her ability to bring historical figures and settings to life, while in her *Sea Witch Voyages*, she subtly weaves in elements of magic, myth, and hauntings, creating an immersive experience that transports readers to a time when ghosts might very well still be walking among the living.

In addition to her historical fiction, Helen has written several short stories, further exploring themes of historical adventure or the supernatural with her signature style.

Whether dealing with the echoes of the past or the weight of lost souls, her stories are as compelling as they are convincing. Through her work, she invites readers into a world where the past never truly lets us go.

Helen started writing as a teenager, but after discovering a passion for history, was published in the UK with her Arthurian *Pendragon's Banner* Trilogy and two Anglo-Saxon novels about the events that led to the 1066 Battle of Hastings, one of which, *The Forever Queen* (USA title – *A Hollow Crown* in the UK) became a *USA Today* best-seller. Her *Sea Witch Voyages* are nautical-based adventures inspired by the Golden Age of Piracy. She also writes the *Jan Christopher* cosy mystery series set during the 1970s, and based around her, sometimes hilarious, years of working as a North London library assistant.

Helen, husband Ron and daughter Kathy moved from London to Devon in January 2013 after a Lottery win on the opening night of the London Olympics, 2012. She spends her time glowering at the overgrown garden and orchard, fending off the geese, helping with the horses and, when she gets a moment, writing the next book...

Helen Hollick

ABOUT KATHY HOLLICK

When not encountering friendly ghosts, Kathy's passion is horses and mental well-being. She started riding at the age of three, had her own Welsh pony at thirteen, and discovered showjumping soon after. Kathy now runs her own Taw River Equine Events, and coaches riders of any age or experience, specialising in positive mindset and overcoming confidence issues via her Centre10 accreditation and Emotional Freedom Technique training. EFT, or 'tapping', uses the body's pressure points to aid calm relaxation and to promote gentle healing around emotional, mental or physical issues.

Kathy lives with her farmer partner, Andrew, in their flat adjoining the main farmhouse. She regularly competes at affiliated British Showjumping, and rides side-saddle ('aside') when she has the opportunity. She produces her own horses, several from home-bred foals.

She also has a fun diploma in Dragons and Dragon Energy, which was something amusing to study during the Covid lockdown.

Kathy riding Saffie (La Rafale) at home © Tony Smith

INTRODUCTION

"Sadly, I don't think a book about *friendly* ghosts will get much traction," suggested an acquaintance. Kindly meant, for almost everyone assumes that ghosts and paranormal entities are hostile and frightening. An assumption perpetuated by intentionally scary stories, religious taboo, movies and TV docu-drama 'haunted house' shows. Non-believers – in many cases, correctly – maintain that supernatural experiences are caused by hallucinations of various kinds, the brain visualising something odd into something explainable, or the results of electronic equipment being conveniently misinterpreted. But there does not seem to be any explanation for the *same* 'ghosts' being seen in the *same* place at different times by different people. And actually, the majority of souls that are encountered by genuine Mediums and Spiritualists are not nasty spooks out to scare us. It's about time that the Hallowe'en image of fear and superstition was firmly set aside. Most ghosts are non-threatening, friendly and indifferent to our presence – or even as unaware of us as most of us are of them.

I am Helen Hollick, and aided by my spiritually gifted daughter Kathy, we set out in this little book to explore the presence of some non-threatening 'ghosts' here in North Devon, where we live. We share our encounters with some of the people who were here before us, whose presence lingers for a variety of reasons, and who mean us no harm.

You either believe in the existence of ghosts or you don't. It depends on whether you've encountered something supernatural or not. 'Seeing is believing' as the saying goes. But when, like us, you share a home with several companionable spirits, or discover benign ghosts in public places who appear as real as any living person, scepticism is abandoned and the myth that ghosts are to be feared is realised as nonsense.

A genuine Medium or Spiritualist will not need to demand, "Is there anyone there?" but will immediately notice a presence and simply offer a welcoming, "Hello."

Here in North Devon, spirits from the past might be encountered where they would be expected – on battle sites, in old pubs and inns, walking the corridors of old houses or lingering on the dockside where tall ships once dropped anchor. But they can also be found beside busy roads, strolling along quiet country lanes, and even keeping an eye on a busy modern car park. And lingering spirits are not limited to people, for animals remain among us as well. It is, I think, comforting to know that our loved ones – human and pets – are, in some way, still with us.

Whether you believe in the supernatural or not is a matter for individual consideration, but for those who have the gift to see, hear or be aware of people from the past, meeting with them in today's environment can generate a connection to years gone by. Those who came before us and who chose to remain among us, whether strangers or relatives and ancestors, are to be welcomed, not feared.

Kathy was nine when she first mentioned 'something

odd'. We were at a re-enactment of the Battle of Hastings at the English Heritage site of Battle Abbey in Sussex where I was researching the history of 1066 for one of my novels. (*Harold the King* UK title / *I Am The Chosen King* US title.) She asked why one of the men was not getting up like the other re-enactors, and when would they remove the dead horse? I made some non-committal answer, but began to wonder when she made the same comments, pointing to the same spots at events in successive years, one of which had no horses in the organised display.

As an adult Kathy saw the same 'bodies' on our last visit in 2012. She knows exactly where King Harold II fell. (English Heritage have got it wrong.)

She says: "I always found it disturbing to walk through the gift shop because many men died in that location in 1066, leaving behind an overpowering smell of blood."

The Battle of Hastings: a Norman re-enactor © *Robin Jacob, film producer*

Many of the encounters related in this narrative are personal in origin, not second-hand anecdotes or over-dramatised (and mostly unbelievable) tales to deliberately scare and frighten. Some of the private locations mentioned are inaccessible to public scrutiny, but there are enough public places, such as old pubs, villages and beaches, for ghost enthusiasts to explore – and maybe experience a friendly encounter or two.

Accompanied by photographs of some of the locations – and animals – featured in the text, *Ghost Encounters* will fascinate all who enjoy this beautiful region of South-West England, as well as interest those who wish to discover more about its history. And a few of its ghosts.

Let's meet some of them...

CHAPTER 1
WELCOME TO NORTH DEVON

Published in three volumes between 1724-1727, Daniel Defoe, the author of *Robinson Crusoe* (and a government spy as a secondary occupation), produced *A Tour Thro' the Whole Island of Great Britain*. South Devon impressed him but North Devon he declared to be, 'Wild, barren and poor.' He was right about the wild landscape, for Exmoor has a natural beauty of dramatic scenery and a rugged, breath-taking coastline that, in the past, saw many a tragic shipwreck.

Devonshire, now known just as Devon, is a large county sought after, today, by people wanting to escape the overcrowding of busy cities, but in the early 1800s most of North Devon was home to poor communities. Rural agriculture was declining and many left for the promise of America and the lure of Californian gold.

The Exmoor coast © Simon Murgatroyd

Home to the famous Cream Tea of scones, clotted cream and jam (cream first, then jam – the other way round is a Cornish tradition, not Devonshire), Devon is the fourth largest county in England with Cumbria – which came into existence when Cumberland and Westmorland were amalgamated in 1974 – taking third place. Devon is unique, however, in having two separate coastlines, one north, one south, and can boast the longest network of roads. (And probably the most potholes.)

Devon shares borders with Somerset, Dorset and Cornwall. Plymouth is the largest city, while Exeter is the county town, with the seaside resorts of Torquay and Paignton along the south coast being popular holiday spots. Ilfracombe and Woolacombe to the north sit alongside the towns of Barnstaple and Bideford.

Geographically, Devon has two moorlands, Dartmoor and Exmoor, with several notable rivers such as the Taw, Torridge, Exe, Mole, and the longest, the Tamar.

Autumn on Exmoor

Exmoor © Tony Smith

North Devon is very different from South Devon, and has a diverse history, especially concerning the old inns and properties; a history which is occasionally revealed by encounters with previous residents or visitors. Sparsely populated during the Iron Age, Roman and Post-Roman periods, it was known as Dumnonia to the Celtic Britons. The Anglo-Saxon *Dyfneint* evolved into the familiar name, Devon, and the area was absorbed into the kingdom of Wessex in the eighth and ninth centuries, with England's first overall King, Æthelstan, setting the Tamar as the boundary with Cornwall in 936. In 1002/3, Exeter was given as dowry to Emma of Normandy when she was married to Æthelred the Unready. By that marriage, King Edward the Confessor was born. In a second marriage, she became the wife of Cnut of Denmark (King Canute of the waves fame). Exeter eventually passed to Edward's widow, Edith, King Harold II's sister, after the Norman Conquest. Harold's mother, Gytha, owned extensive lands in North Devon, from Porlock on the coast down to near where South Molton is located today.

Exeter has served as a highly important trade town from Roman times, while Cornwall's Falmouth, with its third deepest harbour in the world, later becoming an important naval hub. To the north, until the rivers silted up, Barnstaple and Bideford were ports for the wool trade, and the destination for much of the tobacco from Virginia and other American Colonies.

Apart from the dispute over the rightful succession between Stephen of Blois and the Empress Matilda (1138-1153) which only briefly touched Exeter, other English conflicts greatly affected Devon and the West Country, starting with Viking raids from Dublin, through the Norman Conquest, the Wars of the Roses, Perkin Warbeck's rising in 1497 and the English Civil War which split not only those of different political or religious beliefs, but tore individual families apart. The tragic battle at Great Torrington, North

Devon, was one of the last Civil War skirmishes and ultimately led to the final defeat of King Charles I.

The Spanish Armada, during the reign of Queen Elizabeth I, involved Devon's extensive ship building capability, and made famous a chap called Sir Francis Drake, born in Tavistock, c.1540, who reputedly wished to finish his game of bowls in Plymouth before setting sail. (Not that sensational: he could not have sailed until the tide turned!) Sailor and Explorer, Sir Walter Raleigh, also of Tudor fame, was born in Devon.

In the Georgian period, Devon's harbours and coasts were important for trade – legal and illegal, courtesy of numerous smugglers and seafarers. By the Victorian era, when sea bathing was popular and the railways had made travel easy, Devon became popular as a tourist resort, with poets such as Samuel Taylor Coleridge and William Wordsworth gaining inspiration from exploring the wild landscape.

North Devon is predominantly rural, with few large towns dotted amongst scattered villages and farms, which mostly concentrate on dairy or sheep. The Exmoor coast has high, rugged cliffs, the highest, near Combe Martin Bay, being Great Hangman, a 1,043ft hog's-back, with a 820ft cliff-face. The Bristol Channel, merging into the Atlantic, and the west-facing coast of Bideford Bay and Hartland Point peninsula all provide excellent beaches for surfing.

From Celtic to Roman, through the Anglo-Saxons, Vikings and Normans, via the Tudors, Stuarts, Georgians and Victorians North Devon has been rich in its history of the past.

And its ghosts.

CHAPTER 2
WHAT ARE GHOSTS?

Ghost, spirit, shade, presence, spectre, soul – whatever term you prefer to use, unless you are a sceptic the general thinking about ghosts is that these unexplained phenomena are troubled or tormented apparitions which haunt the places where they died. They are misty shapes curling beneath trees, lurking in dark shadows or eerie cellars while oozing an atmosphere of supernatural horror. Spirits allegedly remain through spite or remorse; their only intention is to frighten living people in any and every way they can.

Most of this thinking is generated by religious beliefs and enhanced by the fascination for horror novels and Hollywood movies of the paranormal. Exposing an angry poltergeist or a vengeful demon is common on the TV or cinema screen. Readers and viewers (for some unfathomable reason!) like to be scared. There *are* hostile spirits creating hostile environments, but outside of high drama and the movies, these are in a minority.

Movies such as *Ghostbusters* are not so frightening, but perpetuate the belief that unfriendly ghosts are to be extinguished as soon as possible. A few ghost movies, however, are clever – Clint Eastwood's *Pale Rider* and *High Plains Drifter* spring to mind. *Hamlet*, of course, is a ghost story, as is Dickens' *A Christmas Carol*. The 1945 version of Noel Coward's *Blithe Spirit* starring Rex Harrison and Margaret Rutherford is delightfully amusing. UK TV had its share of entertaining concepts, such as the 1969-1970 *Randall and Hopkirk (Deceased)*, and the children's comedy series, *Rentaghost*, which starred many well known actors of the mid-seventies, such as the delightful Molly Weir, Christopher Biggins and Sue Nicholls, better known, perhaps, for her role as Audrey in *Coronation Street*.

A more recent BBC sitcom series, *Ghosts* (2019-2023), brought further entertainment as adult comedy. The ghosts in this series remain, bored with their repetitive routine, in the house where they died. When new owners arrive, they initially resent the intrusion but then discover the joy of new company and watching television. I often complain that my husband forgets to turn the telly off when he goes out, but now I feel obliged to leave it on in case our resident ghosts were also watching.

A pity they don't pay anything towards our electricity bill.

The Akashic Records are an energy force of emotions, words, thoughts and events which remain as echoes from the past. This echo-energy surrounds us as a permanent memory which can be accessed by those who are able to tune into it. Many 'ghosts' are possibly, therefore, these Akashic Memories, their images seen, felt, or heard as remnants of past lives or events projected into the present like some form of archaic YouTube video system where the replay button is permanently set to 'on'. The majority of 'ghosts' remain in their own time and place, unaware of our presence and are no threat. And just as in a video or TV show, we can see the participating actors, but they cannot see us.

It is natural to have a reaction of fear if something supernatural is encountered, but there is usually no reason to stay frightened. Some, particularly the spirits of children, *can* be mischievous, but aggressive or malevolent hostility, despite what is depicted on TV, is rarely an intentional threat. Some lingering spirits may be confused and bewildered, or even unaware that they are dead, and therefore may need a sympathetic nudge to move on. Quite a few drift among us because they *want* to stay, not because they are trapped, are being punished for some misdemeanour or are intent on intrusive revenge.

Spirits can remain in places where they lived or visited, not necessarily where they died. They stay where they were content and comfortable, or perhaps where particular emotional events happened. Graveyards, outside of Victorian myth, movies and stories are surprisingly lacking in ghostly appearances. Cemeteries really *are* places where to 'rest in peace' is the expected normality.

Are angels ghosts? Ethereal beings seen within a religious – Christian – context? A Guardian Angel may well be a specific spirit who has taken on the task of watching over you. Do we all have such a guardian? Maybe it's just that not all of us are aware of him or her. Whether they are with us or not, I have always adhered to some good advice: *Do not go faster than your guardian angel can fly*.

Sceptics offer many reasons to discredit the existence of ghosts, the gist being that because something cannot be proven then it cannot be true. That is a blinkered argument, and does not explain why the same things – the same ghosts – are seen at the same place by different people, at different times, under different conditions.

After all, where the Universe is concerned, String Theory, Dark Matter and such remain as speculative, *unproven* theories, yet that does not put scientific possibilities into the realm of nonsense. So why should the matter of ghosts be any different?

Descriptions of a ghost or spirit can vary from an unseen but felt presence, a translucent, barely visible shape, or a lifelike form. Most docu-drama supernatural TV shows portray ghosts as anything from an unexplained noise – things that go bump in the night – to something terrifyingly paranormal. Many of these shows are, however, nothing more than excitement-catching pseudoscience-drama. Why are these investigations *always* conducted at night? Spirits are *not* confined to the hours of darkness. (Or do ghost Equity unions forbid daylight appearances on commercial TV?) Darkness, of course, enhances the apprehension and magnifies the fear. What could be normal in daylight can be terrifying at night.

Organised ghost tours are popular and are good fun as the guides involved know their history, are excellent storytellers and provide an evening of interesting entertainment, usually ending at a local hostelry. Devon has several such tours, as do most major towns – London, York, Birmingham, Bath etc. But most ghost tours merely recount exciting stories, and cannot always be taken as legitimate supernatural occurrences.

For most pseudo-encounters, the pleading of, "Is there anyone there?" is a clichéd remnant from the Victorian era when seances and paranormal amusements were popular. Any *genuine* Medium or Spiritualist, such as Kathy, or our friends Vara Hrolfswiffe and Adrienne Hesketh, are automatically aware of a presence and do not need to ask!

Despite an increase in scientific knowledge since the

Victorian age, Ghost Hunting is still a fashionable sport, purely because the phenomenon is unexplained, exciting and, yes, scary. As a hobby the pursuit of the uncanny is harmless; but do keep a large pinch of salt to hand.

A typical team of ghost hunters aim to impress by obtaining 'evidence' of supernatural activity by using a variety of electronic devices. Electronic gadgets do not prove anything. Cold spots, peculiar noises, misty patches and such indicate nothing except cold spots, peculiar noises and misty patches, all of which might be strange but can be explainable occurrences.

Go into a disused railway tunnel or pub cellar after dark and switch on your equipment. You will always pick something up, but those slightly distorted voices are likely to be radio or mobile phone signals. (They carry a long way – even into Space!) Such eerie locations have echoes and damp, mouldy, walls which can affect breathing or muddle cognitive awareness. At the very least, why would any self-respecting ghost want to hang about in these uncomfortable places?

Many natural things can set off an EMF (Electromagnetic Field Detector) but the sources are not ghostly encounters: faulty wiring, nearby phone towers, sunspot activity, or even the feedback from the electrical gadgetry being used can be responsible. Some of this equipment is also extremely detrimental to wildlife; *please don't use them*. Bats in particular have their sensory abilities seriously disrupted.

A genuine person who *can* see and hear ghosts does not need electronic equipment. They encounter spirits under normal circumstances, in normal places, during normal hours. The one thing that can be relied upon where ghost hunting is concerned: anything picked up by electronic equipment is very unlikely to be a ghost.

CHAPTER 3
HOME AND OUR HOUSE GUESTS

Home. The day we moved in, January 2013

An unexpected lottery win on the opening night of the 2012 London Olympics heralded a life-changing 'dream come true' for us. We decided to take the opportunity to leave The Smoke for the rural countryside. Not as daft as it seems, for London living was a necessity, not a choice. Horse owners, dog lovers, cat slaves and country people at heart, we jumped at the chance to get out and pursue a better existence. Friends did warn that we would miss the corner shop, the buses, nightlife and close neighbours. They were wrong. Our village has an adequate community shop, events at the pub and village hall provide entertainment, and the lack of a bus is more than compensated for by the beautiful scenery – and our neighbourly neighbours are not that far away.

Andrew and Kathy. Christmas quiz night, raising money for local charities at the Exeter Inn 2023 © The Exeter Inn

Several location options had been discussed, and Devon was the one we agreed on. Kathy and I felt instantly at ease when we saw what was to be our new home for the first time. This was for BBC TV's *Escape to the Country*, an internationally popular show featuring potential home buyers searching for their dream homes in rural UK areas. Our host was Jonnie

Irwin, now sadly passed away. The first house we were shown ticked all the boxes: old enough to harbour a lot of history, sturdy, stone walls (over three feet deep in places), a 'country-feel' kitchen and the required bedrooms and facilities. Outside, thirteen acres of land, including fields and an orchard, a greenhouse, stables and outbuildings. It was built, we think, in 1769 with old features that define its age and character. I would have signed a cheque there and then.

The *Escape* team returned in 2020 to do a follow-up shoot, this time with Alistair Appleton.

Our Exmoor ponies and Eddie the dog supervise one of the I Escaped to the Country team in 2020

The tingle of recognition from the past and the warm feeling of welcome was obvious the moment we walked into the sitting room, which with its huge stone fireplace incorporating an old bread oven, was once the kitchen, the essential heart of a household.

It was not long after moving in during a snowstorm in January 2013, however, that we realised we were not alone. There are other residents from previous years dwelling alongside us, or encountered around the farm. I wish I could see and hear them myself, but that privilege is for Kathy. All of them are friendly and welcoming, and are regarded by us as our extended family.

THE MAID

Milly-Molly – we're not quite sure of her name – was the first to reveal herself. She is the resident maid, dressed in Georgian-style garments with a lace-trimmed mobcap and spotless apron. She bustles about, keeping an eye on the house, and us, tutting at me when I take the laundry basket out via the *front* door to dry items in the sun. Apparently, in a message passed through Kathy, I should use the *kitchen* door. But I'm forgiven as Milly-Molly is thrilled to be mentioned in a modern book, having only been aware, in her time, of the Bible. She stays here, we were told, because she belongs to the house and it is her duty to take care of it and its inhabitants. I regard our duty is to be as fond of the place as she is.

The dining room where a young boy, the Master and Milly-Molly have been seen. This would originally have been a parlour; the wall with its 'wooden window' is a modern addition

The most delightful sighting of Milly-Molly was one February evening when a friend came to play a few beautiful tunes on his violin. Kathy said nothing until he had gone. "You wouldn't have seen," she announced, "but Milly-Molly and another lady were dancing together outside. They liked the music."

I love the thought that those from the past are sharing, and enjoying, pleasurable occasions along with us.

RESIDENTS OF THE HOUSE

The Master is a large man. (Think The Beast from TV's *The Chase*.) He is a family man who takes great pride in his home, land and livestock. Kathy has seen him in different rooms, on different occasions. He seems to be unaware of our presence, apart from one afternoon a few months after we had moved in. There was a sudden disturbance throughout as if a great wind had burst in, even though it was a warm, sunny afternoon. Our dog, Baz, shaking with fear, slunk into my comforting embrace. Not knowing what had happened, but certain this was something supernatural, I contacted Vara, a Medium friend, who confirmed that the Master had lost his temper and whatever had upset him had reverberated through the dimensions of time. I hadn't mentioned to her about Baz, but she conveyed that the Master was extremely apologetic for alarming me *and the dog*.

During those first few months, Kathy became aware of a presence in one of the bedrooms. A young lady who was no bother, but was sad and lonely. Vara confirmed that the woman was in her early twenties and was an orphan; the family was close kindred, hence, had taken her in. Because of her orphan status I immediately named her 'Jane' for poor Jane Eyre, although there, any similarity ended.

"She is treated well and kindly," Vara confirmed, "with nothing to want for, but she is always aware that her aunt and uncle are not her parents, and her cousins are not her siblings. She is alone a lot of the time in her room, reading her Bible and keeping herself to herself."

I gathered from this that 'Jane' was deeply grieving, so I decided to notice her in ways that I could. I put fresh flowers on her bedroom windowsill and made a point of saying good morning and good night to her every day. After about a month we realised that her presence was no longer there, so she has moved on to rest peacefully alongside her loving family.

All she wanted was for someone to notice her and to care.

Undoubtedly farmers, the Master and Mistress lived here probably from when the house was built in 1769 until the mid-1800s. Was the house built for them, a young, newly married couple? The house was rented, not their own, and possibly belonged to the neighbouring, larger farm. They seem to have been good people, financially secure and very much in love with each other, which explains why the atmosphere of our house is such a happy one. Vara told us that when a new maid arrived wearing old boots that were worn and leaked, the Master promptly bought her a new pair. Was this our Milly-Molly? It would explain why she remains here, and so obviously adores the place.

Love and laughter filled the house then, and as present-day guardians we try to keep the same welcoming, happy, atmosphere. I like to think that those from the past watch, not too critically, as we continue centuries-old tasks such as tending the livestock and haymaking.

Kathy has seen a young boy in various rooms, farmhands in our sitting room (the original kitchen), and Milly-Molly bustling about anywhere and everywhere.

The front door – a couple of dragons and Baz

FARMHANDS AND VISITORS

Outside, Jack is a farmhand seen in the old dairy – a very polite man. I was talking with Vara at 10.30 p.m. one August evening in the lane by our front gate. She suddenly stopped talking to me and said, looking towards the dairy, "Thank you for your concern, but we are fine."

Puzzled, I asked, "What was that all about?"

"There's a man leaning on the stable door to the dairy and he is concerned that we are out late unescorted. He enquired whether we needed assistance."

This does show that many spirits care about our welfare. It is a pity that stories of these kind souls do not get mentioned on ghost hunting programmes.

The old dairy, where Jack, the dairyman, still lingers

Wonky Donk. He loved Hobnob biscuits

I often say hello to Jack when I go into the dairy, and there was many an occasion when our dear old donkey, Wonky Donk, now departed from us and who was stabled there, would bray for no reason. I'm certain that he was calling to his friend, Jack. Alternatively, it could be that Wonky Donk loved McVitie's Hobnobs, which I regularly went out to give him as a treat. So maybe he was just shouting for another biscuit?

A village friend, Heather, while visiting for afternoon tea has seen the outline of an elderly lady standing near our front gate. The image was a little fuzzy, but Heather caught a glimpse of a long dress and her hair up in a style that,

"Looked like a cottage loaf, puffed out at the sides with a knob-type bun on top."

We think Kathy has seen this woman in a comfortable chair in the sitting room. Heather has also noticed "A misty shape," in the corner of the room.

THE GEORGIAN DELIVERY MAN

Seen mostly from the waist up, a male, usually wearing a three-corner, 'cocked' hat and a neatly tied lace cravat is an occasional visitor.

During the 1700s to early 1900s there was a thriving catalogue order service from England's expanding midlands industries of the textile mills, furniture makers and the Staffordshire potteries. These catalogues were popular, often accompanied by miniature doll's-house-sized replicas, with small samples provided for fabrics. The goods were often shipped by sea or canal because the roads were rough tracks which made haulage slow and difficult. Our visitor appears to be the equivalent of today's Amazon Delivery Man, transporting goods that arrived by boat at Barnstaple or Bideford.

The first time Kathy met this man, he was in the stableyard. "I looked up and saw him, dressed in old-fashioned clothing, leaning on the yard gate watching me. I thought he was a neighbour, then realised that our neighbours do not wear lace cravats or three-corner hats. When he became aware that I had seen him, he vanished. I think he must have been aged about thirty, not a young man, nor old."

Another time I was watching Kathy ride in the manège.

"There's someone at the gate," she said as she rode past

me. I turned to look. "*You* will not be able to see him," she laughed, "it's our nice delivery man!"

It seems that he comes often, and enjoys observing the horses. Especially, he has conveyed to Vara: "I like the big chestnut," meaning Kathy's showjumper, Shinglehall Casino – stable name, Lexie. He knows a good horse when he sees one.

Kathy riding Lexie (Shinglehall Casino) side-saddle in her green velvet, Napoleonic War Championship-winning costume

The man's name is William, "Named for the King," he told Vara. But *which* King William? There were four. We need to investigate some clues:

Vara tracked him to the house, delivering a large wooden crate which, mystified, the Mistress began unpacking – and promptly burst into delighted tears. Her husband had ordered a surprise present; an entire dinner service of Ironstone Chinaware, packed in layers of straw and sawdust.

Ironstoneware was originally produced by the Staffordshire potteries as a cheaper alternative to bone china. Ironstone is a form of sedimentary rock, but its impurities make it useless as a ceramics component. The name, however, implies strength and a resistance to cracking or chipping. Antique ironstoneware is now highly collectable. I have a cup and saucer made by Davenport Potteries, an English manufacturer of tableware based in Staffordshire between 1794 and 1887, with Ironstone being produced soon after 1800. Speculative, but maybe my cup and saucer are similar to that unexpected gift? They at least date to the right period of the late 1700s to early 1800s for our delivery man.

Davenport Potteries. Ironstoneware cup and saucer

Master William's hat is another clue. The turn of the century was a transitional period for fashion for both sexes. For the last years of the 1790s the tricorn or cocked hat (called a three-corner in the early 1700s), would still have been worn, but by 1800 it was becoming a hat of the past for any fashionable gent, replaced by a 'top', 'silk' or 'beaver' hat, depending on what material used, although prior to 1793 no top hats would have been worn as they did not exist before that date. More traditional men, those of rural counties, of limited financial means or plain not bothered by fashion, would stay with what they were comfortable wearing, so the tricorn was around for several more years. Viewers of BBC TV's recent *Poldark* series set between 1781 and 1801 and starring Aiden Turner, would have seen this clearly, for Ross Poldark continued to wear his tricorn while the more affluent George Warleggan changed to the new silk hat.

Given his tricorn hat, William might be making his deliveries in the early 19th century, but we still don't know *which* King William he was named after when he was born, estimated at about 1770.

William I and II can be ruled out for these are from the 11th century: Duke William of Normandy and his son, William Rufus. William III is better known as William of Orange, a Dutchman married to Mary, niece to King Charles II, and the Protestant daughter of the king's disliked Catholic brother James, who became King James II. William and Mary reigned as joint monarchs from 1689 to 1702 after James was deposed, so a little early for our man? But a possibility?

King William IV, born in 1765 at Buckingham House (eventually better known as Buckingham Palace), reigned from 1830-1837. His main claim to fame being that he was succeeded by his only living relative, his eighteen-year-old niece, Victoria, although several notable reforms were made during his short reign: child labour was restricted and slavery abolished through most of the British Empire. But ... he is not right for our William.

So, is King William of Orange, a staunch Protestant, our man's namesake? One reason is this King's connection with Devon. He invaded England in what became known as the Glorious Revolution, landing at Brixham, South Devon in 1688 and James II fled into exile shortly after.

Prior to this, the Monmouth Rebellion of 1685 had ravaged the West Country during an attempt to remove James as King. Believing that he had the right to the throne, the illegitimate son of Charles II, James Scott, Duke of Monmouth, aimed to topple his uncle but was defeated at Sedgemoor in Somerset, near the Devon border. Monmouth was executed and the Bloody Assizes followed, presided over by Judge Jeffreys who hanged many of the surviving anti-

Catholic rebels and their innocent family members. Even a century later the memory of those fearful times remained with the people of Somerset and Devon, with William of Orange remembered as a popular king by those of the Protestant faith.

William III died in 1702 of pneumonia, following a broken collarbone after a fall from Sorrel, his horse, which had stumbled into a mole's hole. For many years after, Jacobite supporters toasted 'the little gentleman in the black velvet waistcoat', meaning the innocent mole.

Was this the king remembered, and honoured, by our William's parents?

A view of the Taw Valley

All spirits who visit or continue to reside here at our farm, are friendly and offer no harm whatsoever, but a new chap did cause Kathy some consternation. It is unconventional to have a ghost hoping for a mental therapy session.

She awoke in the early hours one winter morning to feel a weight sitting on her bed. A small, stocky man with rough whiskers, desperately wanted to talk to her. Getting the impression that the chap – Reginald or Roger, she thinks – had special needs of some sort, she talked to him for some while. Although awake and aware of her exact surroundings, she has little memory of the somewhat incoherent conversation. Dreams can often seem like this, but in hindsight you realise the anomalies – discrepancies in the room regarding perspective, furniture or layout, or everything back to front. This was no dream.

The next day Kathy had stern words with her visitor telling him he is most welcome to come and chat, but *not* during the night and most definitely *not* in her bedroom. Since then the floorboards on the landing and stairs have unaccountably creaked, but the man himself has not reappeared. We think that he was from the village, and looking for assurance and a chance to talk. Kathy, being an accredited mental health therapist, may have triggered him seeking her assistance for whatever was troubling him.

Kathy would like to know who the man is – was – but might have to wait until he visits again, more politely. Unless anyone local can shed light upon who he might be?

One frosty morning in late November 2023, Kathy saw, quite clearly, a man sitting on the trunk of an old tree that had fallen down many years ago, but was still alive and healthy despite its recumbent position. He was wearing a green Barbour coat and a flat cap. Kathy had been up to the yard feeding the horses their breakfast and thought the man was Andrew, her partner.

"What are you doing sitting there in the cold?" she asked, surprised, only to realise that Andrew was standing beside the Landrover on the opposite side of the lane. When Kathy looked back, the sitting man had gone.

Former neighbour, Tony, had moved away several years previously, but had, as we subsequently discovered, died in January 2023. I mentioned this unexplained appearance in my monthly website journal and a few weeks later received an email response from Tony's partner, Diane Lang.

"The description of the man in the green Barbour and flat cap fits Tony exactly!" she explained.

The lane to both properties is shared access, so Tony and Diane would often walk their two Labradors past our house, with this particular fallen tree being an ideal place to catch breath after trudging up the hill. Diane went on to say, "Tony was always so very happy at our farm, I would like to think his spirit was visiting old familiar places." She added: "Give him my love if he visits again,"

With great pleasure, we certainly will.

Tony and his beloved Labradors © Diane Lang

CHAPTER 4
CLOSE TO HOME

Ghosts and spirits can be encountered anywhere at any time. Kathy has 'met' people along busy roads and in narrow Devonshire lanes. And not just people. She has seen several animals, the most impressive of which is a sabre-toothed Big Cat in our woods. None of these encounters worry us, except Kathy admits that coming across a dinosaur of any variety would not be appreciated.

The high hedges of a Devonshire lane

A few miles from South Molton and not far from Exmoor, our village of Chittlehamholt is part of the North Devon parish of Chittlehamholt, Satterleigh and Warkleigh. We have twenty-six Grade II listed buildings which include various houses and farm buildings and The Exeter Inn, a 16th -century coaching inn. The village is reached by typical Devonshire lanes which are notoriously narrow and twisty, their high, protective hedges atop centuries-old banks formed safe tracks for moving cattle and sheep, and provided secretive routes for smugglers to transport contraband. They can be a bit of a nightmare for the modern motorist, however, especially when needing to reverse.

Chittlehamholt c.1900. Reproduced from the original by kind permission © Richard Lethbridge

Chittlehamholt: the view in the other direction c.1900.
Reproduced from the original by kind permission © Richard Lethbridge

Kathy has encountered deceased local farmers and farmhands in the lanes and on nearby properties. A few are recognisable, but as present-day families still live in the area some names and locations must remain private.

One old farmer was leaning on a fence in the village inspecting the stock – nothing unusual about that except he had passed away a few weeks beforehand. Another time Kathy heard a voice advise: "Take your time, don't 'urry 'em." This was to a neighbour farmer attempting to sort some fractious calves.

A Taw Valley farm lane, complete with a shallow ford

North Devon is predominantly a dairy farming and sheep rearing county

IN THE TRENCHES

On Remembrance Sunday 2023, Kathy had been watching *War Horse* at a friend's house. The scenes in this film are very poignant and she became aware of a shadowy figure standing nearby. The shadow became more solid and a male voice said, very quietly, "'Tweren't like that. 'Twere louder, noisier." Kathy had the distinct impression of a young First World War soldier and soon realised that this was Harry, who died on active service on March 16th 1917. Kathy then heard him say that the rats were bad, and the men kept cats to keep them down. "The cats," he explained, "were a comfort."

Detail from 'Trench Pals – a brew, a fag, and a good companion. Flanders 1916' reproduced by kind permission © Chris Collingwood, historical artist

With later research we discovered that about 500,000 cats inhabited the entire structure of the trenches. Rat traps were impractical to use because of the mud and water; the cats did a better job and also served as mascots and friends. As with canaries in mines, cats were immediately susceptible to toxic invisible gases, their reaction alerting the men to put on their gas masks. It is not known how many cats died, but their presence saved many soldiers' lives.

'The Burning Moment. The Somme, July 1st 1916', reproduced by kind permission © Chris Collingwood, historical artist

Neither I nor Kathy were aware, before this revelation, that cats were there with the men. Thank you, Harry, for telling us about them.

Church bells rang out when the war was officially ended. The last words Harry spoke to Kathy were sad. In a quiet voice he murmured: "I never heard those bells."

He was only twenty years old, and is buried in Gorre British and Indian Cemetery, France. RIP Harry.

To Memory Ever Dear.
   Private Harry Bater.
   Born: 1897 in Barnstaple, Devon.
   Died: in Active Service 16 March 1917 of Wounds. Aged 20.
   Duty Location: France and Flanders.

From a photograph in a local history book, Kathy recognised Harry and another soldier who had been a regular visitor to our friends' farm as a lad. Both still like to visit.

THE EXETER INN, CHITTLEHAMHOLT

The Exeter Inn, so named because it was the first stop on the coaching route from Barnstaple to Exeter, is a Grade II listed inn built in the 16th century, extended in the 1980s, and again during the later part of the Covid pandemic with an outside deck seating area added by Hazel and Steve Bowles who took the pub over in 2019. Built of roughcast rendered stone and cob, and a recently rethatched roof adorned by a cheeky fox stalking two pheasants, The Exeter Inn now boasts several well-deserved awards.

The Exeter Inn, a welcoming and friendly hub of the village © The Exeter Inn

There was also an Exeter Inn situated in Litchdon Street, Barnstaple, dating back to about the same time, and another in South Street, South Molton, which leads to speculation that perhaps these were all connected coaching stops en route to Exeter?

Dog friendly: Frankie welcomes all visitors – past and present!
© The Exeter Inn

Regular coach travel had been used by private, wealthy, owners since the Tudor age of the 1500s; before then getting about had mostly been by sea, on horseback, or by foot. The stagecoach became a popular mode of public transport in the late 1600s when regular routes were installed with travel from one 'stage' to the next, usually a distance of about eight to fifteen miles depending on the terrain. By the Georgian era of the 1800s coaching routes often had four coaches per route, two in each direction two or three times a week. On more popular routes this increased to once a day.

At each stop, usually an established inn, the horses would be changed and the passengers and coachman have a chance for a comfort break, or if a longer stop, a meal, drink and overnight accommodation. Travel would be slow at a speed of about ten miles an hour, taking about eight days in the 1670s to reach London from Exeter. One old coaching firm claimed that they went from London to Exeter in three days, but this was an advertising exaggeration, for everyone knew it took nearer six.

The Exeter Inn became part of the public network of coaches around 1705 and today, The Exeter Inn is a lively pub offering food, drink and a warm welcome – and resident guests from the past who continue to enjoy the friendly ambience, although one group of men are in difficulties. They are King Charles I's Royalists – Cavaliers, dishevelled, weary, wounded and in desperate need of remounts...

'A Brief Respite – A Troop of Royalist Harquebusiers 1645', reproduced by kind permission © Chris Collingwood, historical artist

THE BATTLE OF TORRINGTON, FEBRUARY 16TH 1646

Great Torrington (often locally just called Torrington), is rarely referred to in accounts of the English Civil War, but it saw a decisive engagement which ended the campaign in the West Country and, ultimately, the war itself. England had endured the upheaval of civil war since 1642, with the supporters of King Charles I and the Catholic Church fighting against Parliamentarians (Roundheads), commanded by Sir Thomas Fairfax alongside Oliver Cromwell's New Model Army, which mostly consisted of men who held a Puritan belief. At the heart of the division between religious and political opinion, even within families, was the right of the sovereign to rule by Divine Right versus government by Parliament. A division which tore the country apart and was to end with the public execution of King Charles I in January 1649.

By 1646 Fairfax and Cromwell had advanced into the south-west. Tiverton had fallen and Royalist Exeter was besieged. In the February, commanded by Lord Hopton, the king's men moved up from Cornwall to North Devon and occupied the strategically important town of Great Torrington. Fairfax abandoned the Exeter siege and marched with 10,000 men to reach Torrington on the 16th. He decided to wait until the next day to attack the extensive defence barricades surrounding the town, but Lieutenant-General Cromwell believed that the Royalists were planning to move out, so he and Fairfax launched an immediate full assault.

Two hours of fighting at the barricades followed, resulting in the outnumbered Royalist infantry becoming overwhelmed. They retreated into the town, while their cavalry attempted to counter-attack along Torrington's narrow streets.

Something, or someone, ignited one of the Royalist's eighty barrels of gunpowder stored in the crypt below the church. The subsequent explosion destroyed the church and surrounding area, killing or injuring many, including captured prisoners held inside the church. Fairfax himself narrowly escaped serious injury from falling masonry and pieces of lead. The noise from the explosion must have been tremendous. The hills and valleys along the River Taw would have carried the sound for miles.

The disaster ended the battle. The remnants of the king's men fled, with, we assume, a small group who sought aid at The Exeter Inn, ten or so miles away.

Kathy has seen and heard these men on several occasions. The first encounter was with local author, Robert Hesketh and his spiritually gifted wife, Adrienne, who were researching several Devon inns for Robert's book *Haunted Inns of Exmoor and North Devon*. We joined them one afternoon at The Exeter Inn, and it turned out to be very interesting.

'Royalist Officer of Horse King's Army 1643', reproduced by kind permission © Chris Collingwood, historical artist

The Royalist Captain, Richard – we have not discovered his surname – wears a red coat, breeches and boots. He has a cavalryman's sword at his hip and is leaning against the pub's mantelpiece, a pewter tankard of ale in his trembling hand. His face is ash pale and dirt-smeared beneath his flop of dishevelled blond hair and ragged beard. His clothes are muddy and torn, his knuckles and fingers are bleeding. Bravely, he tries to ignore the wound which is troubling him beneath the material of his blood-stained cummerbund.

Another, not so clearly seen man is standing nearby. He is equally muddied, bedraggled and anxious. A third, just as begrimed, weary and bloodstained, wearing a dark blue coat sits at a table nursing a tankard of ale and smoking a long-stemmed clay pipe. There is a strong smell of hops and tobacco in the air, mixed with crushed lavender from the rushes covering the floor. The pipe smoker's name might be Cedric or Cecil.

A fourth man, dressed in a muddied green coat, paces anxiously up and down, eager to be gone and away to safety. His name is possibly Mervyn. If the enemy catches them, they will become prisoners, or hanged. But how can they flee any further? One of their horses is dead, another is severely lame.

The landlord, obviously a king's man, has sent word for aid. Can anyone nearby help? Horses are needed urgently. If he is found sheltering these men his inn will be destroyed. Then Kathy saw a boy of about ten run in, heard him shout that horses were found – a farmer will exchange two of his sturdy farm cobs for the lame mare. A bargain as the mare is well bred, hide her away somewhere, breed from her: a good exchange.

A question arose from Steve, the present-day landlord, who had been listening intently to Kathy and Adrienne conversing together, each lady seeing the same scene but from different perspectives.

"Why," he asked, "can we see these soldiers? They seem to have been here for only a short while, and did not die here?"

"I think," Kathy answered, "that we are eavesdropping on an echo of something deeply emotional, something with an intense strength of stored energy. It is like watching a YouTube video that is replaying an important memory that has been imprinted here through extreme anxiety and stress."

Two years later, in February 2024, Kathy and I again met with Robert and Adrienne in The Exeter Inn for a congenial lunch, and a 'ghostly' catch up. The troop were again seen by both ladies, but this time the shy trooper revealed himself. He is dressed in brown and is standing in the present-day 'doorway' (an open gap) which leads to the toilets. Two more troopers, wearing mustard-coloured coats, were also seen on this occasion.

However, that is not the end of the story. There is more to tell at another inn a few miles away in King's Nympton...

THE GROVE INN, KING'S NYMPTON

King's Nympton is a village and parish about four miles south-south-west of the town of South Molton. The Grove is an award-winning, welcoming, Grade II listed thatched inn, situated in the heart of the village. With low beams, flagstone floors and a roaring fire in winter, the inn offers a friendly atmosphere, local ales and an excellent menu. (Which we can attest to from several family outings.) But one visit in particular in September 2023 had us excited, and intrigued. A familiar ghost was there also.

The Grove Inn, King's Nympton. Welcoming and friendly to all visitors © The Grove Inn

At the time of the English Civil War, Sir Hugh Pollard, 2nd Baronet (1603 - November 1666) of King's Nympton was an English soldier and MP who supported the Royalist cause. Serving with the king's army in Devonshire and Cornwall he became Governor of Dartmouth in 1645, but when Fairfax's parliamentary troops besieged the town that year, Pollard was captured and fined £518, almost £100,000 in today's money, which is probably why, in 1653, he sold his manor at King's Nympton when Oliver Cromwell was Lord Protector of England, and the rightful king, Charles II, was exiled in France.

On the evening of our visit, The Grove was busy, and there was an additional, unexpected patron standing near our table. Leaning against the stone wall behind us was Richard, the *same* Cavalier Captain that Kathy had seen at The Exeter Inn. As blood-stained, dishevelled and weary as he had looked at Chittlehamholt.

Purely conjecture: were Captain Richard and his troop Sir Hugh Pollard's men? It is entirely feasible that they were; King's Nympton was, after all, where Pollard had his manor, where there might be horses, assistance, friendly faces and a chance to rest safely.

The riddle: did our tired and injured group of cavalrymen go to The Grove Inn and Pollard's estate first, looking for help, or to The Exeter Inn first? My hunch is they initially went to King's Nympton. Unable to find horses – Sir Hugh would not have been at his manor, maybe no one was there – the men struggled on to the next possible place of assistance, The Exeter Inn, Chittlehamholt.

From there, with replacement mounts and new hope did they get away to safety? I doubt we will ever know, but I hope they did.

MORE FROM THE EXETER INN

Because of its welcoming atmosphere for the living and those who have passed on (and for its delicious food), our local pub is a busy place. The landlords and members of staff, not forgetting Frankie the pub dog, and the cat, have frequently witnessed glasses, wall-hangings and ornaments being moved or taking an inexplicable dive to the floor. Hazel and Steve took over as landlords in the summer of 2019, the building being in poor repair having stood empty for a few years. The new owners moved in and transformed a neglected old place into the lively heart of village life that it has now become, despite the difficulties of the Covid pandemic. Hazel's expertly managed take-away meals were greatly appreciated by villagers during lockdown.

There had not previously been reports of anything supernatural about the pub, but the atmosphere changed to one of open welcome when Steve and Hazel took over.

Steve says, "One evening after closing, Hazel and I were sitting on the settee drinking a relaxing glass of wine when a shadowy shape flew across the room above us. We exclaimed together, 'What was that?' so we both saw it. Then some of the Christmas decorations started bobbing and moving. We think it might have been a spirit playing tricks on us."

For ourselves, the first meeting with Adrienne Hesketh at the pub brought Kathy's previously elementary spiritual ability into full bloom. Sitting chatting together, the two ladies saw several people from bygone eras. Whether these are ghosts or Akashic energy memories is immaterial, for Kathy's encounters then, and several times subsequently, are interesting and cover several centuries from the Elizabethan Tudor age, to the 1950s and '60s.

Some of the ghosts discovered that afternoon with Robert and Adrienne and seen by Kathy since, show the same or similar scenes from the past, while others have appeared to her in today's environment.

Let's work backwards in time...

Seated to the far right of the main bar, beside what is now a very pleasant conservatory, are a group of ladies gathered around a table. From their dress they belong to the 1950s, and this seems to be a regular way that they meet for a light drink and a heavy gossip. It was not until 1982 that women had the legal right to buy themselves a drink at the bar of an English pub. Many pubs would not permit unaccompanied women into the main bar area, instead, they were allotted a separate lounge bar, or a 'snug'. These six ladies at The Exeter Inn all wear hats and are smartly dressed, with the matriarch of the group an older woman who reminded Kathy of the character Nora Batty in BBC TV's comedy series, *Last of the Summer Wine*. The lady is giving the impression of superiority by smoking a cigarette, using a long, black cigarette holder.

They are a garrulous group, talking about a young man

from the village, agreeing that, "He won't make much of himself," and exchanging uncomplimentary opinions about him.

The women are trying to give the aura of refined elegance, sipping from small glasses, drinking what looks and smells like cherry wine, a smooth, full-flavoured sweet wine with a strong cherry aroma, which both Kathy and Adrienne could distinctly identify.

One of the group is younger, recently married. Kathy had the impression that she had been dragged along either by her mother or mother-in-law. She stands out, not because of her younger age, but she is dressed in brighter, more fashionable post-war clothes – a pale pink summer dress and a chic hat. She is also giving an air of feeling decidedly awkward among these patronising older gossips. She tries several excuses to leave, but is over-ruled, in particular by the woman who is dominating the group. Kathy sensed that the young lady would not remain in the village for long, that she would move away with her husband to somewhere less parochial.

We were to meet with the Battleaxe again on a different occasion. Enjoying a delicious family meal seated in the area where the Gossip Group had sat, Kathy began to feel uncomfortable and realised that she was sitting where the Matriarch was customarily ensconced. The feeling of condescension washed over and through Kathy, accompanied by a sneering voice: *You do not even know my name!*

It was later that the name 'Eliza' came into Kathy's mind, and interestingly, she hasn't seen the woman since. However, Kathy *has* encountered one of the other ladies of the group at a different location – standing at the window of one of the village farmhouses. We have tracked her down as Mrs Ellis, distinctive because she had a patch over one eye.

This group of ladies were not exclusively visible to Kathy and Adrienne. Some weeks later a child was eating a meal with his family at the same table, but he was not enjoying himself. When Mum asked what was wrong, he replied that the old lady kept telling him off, and that he didn't like her. Naturally, Mum could see no old lady, but the boy was quite upset. On further questioning, it became clear that this was most definitely Grumpy Eliza.

Landlord Steve has seen Eliza himself. She has given him several frosty stares of a morning. Kathy advised him to politely say, "Good morning," and then ignore her.

Children often see spirits, and we grown-ups tend to put their chattered experiences down to imaginary friends. One quiet afternoon at The Exeter Inn, the child of a member of staff was happily playing where the smithy was once located. Mum could hear the child laughing and talking. When asked to explain who else had been there, the child replied, "The girl." Needless to say, there had been no present-day girl there. Perhaps we ought to take note of what children tell us more often?

Kathy has encountered fleeting glimpses of other customers: an agitated young man pacing up and down, holding forth with his own importance. She says, "I didn't like him much, he was self-opinionated and fond of his own voice." She has only seen him the once, and cannot remember what clothes he wore, although he was from a past century.

There is a group of Edwardian farmers sitting drinking ale at one of the tables in the corner of the main bar, opposite the fireplace. They are dressed in work clothes, farmers' apparel. One man, the main spokesman of the group, is emphasising his point by gesticulating with his pipe – Kathy could smell the tobacco smoke. Standing beside the table is a more elegantly dressed man, maybe a local squire? Tall, dark-haired, with a neatly trimmed beard, a cravat, smart coat, knee-length breeches, long leather boots and holding a riding crop.

Hedges, as well as lanes mark the boundaries between farms and land

The men are vigorously debating the matter of ownership of fields, and establishing the correct boundaries. Even today, unmarked hereditary boundaries can be a sore point between farmers and incomers. The impression received by Kathy and Adrienne was that the 'squire' wanted to purchase some extra land from the pipe-smoking farmer who was having none of it, as he knew the field was in a strategically important position, making it financially valuable.

Did that farmer hold out for the price he wanted, or did the Squire eventually beat him down?

Another grumpy man was spotted by Kathy and Adrienne. He was sitting at the present bar, but made it quite plain that he did not want to participate in any paranormal speculation and promptly disappeared. Both ladies thought he was from the 1960s.

Now a comfortable dining area, but previously a forge where the blacksmith worked © The Exeter Inn

In the lower dining area behind the huge chimney breast and log burner, another scene from the past unfolded for

Kathy and Adrienne to observe. This had once been a lean-to type area with a sloping thatched roof covering what was the smithy. Because of our own horses Kathy is familiar with the smells and sounds of a farrier at work and recognised them instantly.

The forge and anvil are where the fireplace is now situated, and on many occasions when seated in this area eating a meal or enjoying the pub's monthly quiz nights, Kathy has noticed the distinct aroma of shoeing a horse. The tools the blacksmith was using were more or less the same as those of today, the only difference, modern forges are heated by oil, gas or electric power.

The blacksmith was an important person at a coaching inn, and this young chap appeared to be good at his job, but preferred to keep himself to himself. In the revealed scene, he is busy shoeing a farm horse, more interested in what he is doing than taking notice of a group of young village ladies standing to one side, chattering and giggling. One of the group, a blonde, is over-dressed in her finery, attempting to gain his attention.

He, however, thinks they are a nuisance. He is desperate to have a private moment in order to speak to a young lady standing apart from the others, but he is too shy to initiate a conversation. She is pretty, with brown hair and hazel eyes, more plainly and suitably attired in a brown dress with a white chemise. She also wants to speak to the smith, and eventually plucks up courage to talk to him – about the horse. Losing interest the giggling girls depart, much to the smith's relief. He is happy to chat to the young lady about his job, and finally asks if he might be so bold as to walk out with her?

Blushing, she accepts.

Further back in time Kathy caught a glimpse of a man in late Tudor or early Stuart apparel: a cloak, a smallish ruff around his neck, but the glimpse was too fleeting to capture more detail. She did, however, see him again on a different occasion. Definitely from the Tudor period, he wears expensive clothes, velvets and brocades, with delicate but intricate embroidery on his tunic and sleeves. He is with a woman, equally well dressed, her gown, hair and fingers sparkling with pearls and jewels. He is showing her off with great pride, and Kathy had the impression, on both occasions, that he is a nobleman or titled gentleman of some repute, and that they were newly married.

Her additional impression was that they had come from Barnstaple or Bideford and this was the first stopping point to rest the horses, their transport being a private coach. Kathy has seen the couple a few times since, but never as clearly as on that second occasion.

The congenial atmosphere of The Exeter Inn, where a Tudor gentleman shows off his new bride, a group of tired Cavaliers are paused in time and Nancy occasionally gets up to mischief © The Exeter Inn

When Kathy and I met a second time with Robert and Adrienne, the pub was busy with fellow partakers of lunch, and so guests from the past were not so easy to pick up. Shadowy presences were around, but not clear. However, we were eventually rewarded.

The Cavalier Troop were again present, and a few new visitors were discovered. An indistinct lady was sitting in the corner eating a meal but she disappeared when present-day guests sat at the same table. A shadowy shape had been sighted by other people near the back stairs, a shape reluctant to reveal itself to Adrienne and Kathy, but both saw it as a furtive male; a dark-clad man of poor appearance, maybe a vagrant or tramp? Adrienne thought he was a poacher – possibly confirmed when we learnt that another sighting by someone else had been of a headless shape, while another thought the man had been hanged – not at or in the pub, but close by. Adrienne picked up marks on his neck and throat, distinctive indications of severe bruising from a noose. Kathy felt her throat tighten as if something was strangling her, and then had the strong feeling that the shadowy figure didn't want her to see him. Could this be because we own a farm and are friends with local farmers and landowners? A poacher would not be keen to reveal himself to us.

Hanging before the late 1800s was a barbaric process where the condemned victim stood on a barrel, stool or the back of a cart placed beneath the erected gallows. Once the victim was 'Pushed off' the noose tightened around the neck, slowly strangling. It could take up to twenty minutes to die. Relatives or sympathetic friends could hasten the ordeal by rushing forward to add their weight to the victim's dangling torso, a practice which led to the common term 'hangers on' which carries a less sinister connotation these days.

A present-day lady came and sat by herself at a table to enjoy lunch. Adrienne and Kathy now had to talk quietly so as not to be overheard. They did not want to alarm customers! Sitting next to this lady was a short, stout, Gentleman Farmer with a distinctive bulbous nose and florid face. He wore a wing-collared shirt beneath his jacket and had placed his hat behind his chair. He was tucking into a roast dinner with as much gusto as the 21st-century lady next to him. Discreetly, Kathy asked Steve if he knew who the lady was. We did laugh! She was his mum, and when we explained the ghost's presence, she was delighted to discover that she had been joined by a secret companion.

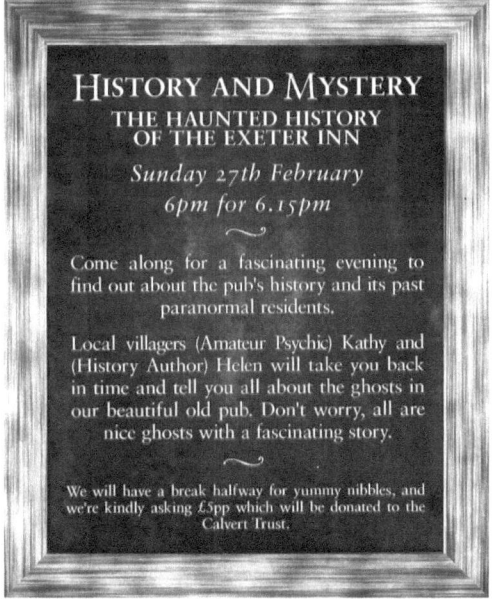

A History and Mystery evening at the pub © Graphic designed from the original by avalongraphics.org

THE STAR OF THE PUB: MEET NANCY

There is one regular visitor to mention, and we're hoping she will be pleased with her star spotlight. Nancy, as we believe she is called, is usually around at The Exeter Inn, although she does not always show herself. Nancy is aged about eleven or twelve, is often up to mischief or enjoying listening to our modern conversations. Occasionally, if no one is noticing her presence, she ruffles wall hangings, or moves chairs. On one occasion during Sunday lunch, landlord Steve was asked by a customer about a particular picture on the wall. Kathy could see Nancy earwigging nearby, and when the customer left, watched as Nancy climbed onto a stool to study the picture for herself.

Nancy was the first spirit Kathy saw soon after Steve and Hazel took the inn over. That first encounter, Nancy was kneeling at a window anxiously looking out for someone, whether in her own time or ours we have no way of knowing. She has loose brown hair down to her shoulders, and wears a plain frock, with a white pinafore. It is not easy to pinpoint Nancy's period, for this was common children's attire from Georgian to Edwardian times.

For some many months Nancy was not seen at all and we wondered if she had moved on. One evening Kathy and I gave a talk about the ghosts of the pub to a packed audience, Kathy speaking about the ghosts, me filling in the history. In mid-flow Kathy stopped, nodded, smiled and said, "Yes, I'll be with you in a moment."

I wondered who she was talking to. We finished the section then Kathy explained.

"I have a rather irate young lady standing in front of me, she is frowning and has her hands on her hips, disgruntled because I haven't mentioned her yet. Ladies and gentleman, I have the honour of introducing you all to Nancy!"

Smiling now, Nancy turned and waved.

It is a great pity that Kathy is, apparently, the only one who can see her, so if you are visiting The Exeter Inn and you also meet Nancy, do let us know.

Or if a picture inexplicably becomes aslant or a glass falls over even though no one is nearby, smile and say hello. It will be Nancy trying to get your attention.

Leaving, or entering, the village of an evening take a moment to glance at the memorial bench near the Mole Resort. You might glimpse a man wearing a flat cap sitting there, admiring the view across the valley.

CHAPTER 5
OUT AND ABOUT

THE MAN IN THE ROAD

What can be disconcerting when being out with Kathy is that she sees people who, to everyone else, are not there but to her are ordinary, living persons. The situation reminds me of A.A. Milne's poem: *The other day upon the stair, I met a man who wasn't there...* This is even more disconcerting when driving up a narrow lane heading for home and she suddenly shouts: "Mind that man!"

"What man?"

"The one in the hi-vis jacket walking down the middle of the road."

The driver of the car coming the other way clearly didn't see this man either, otherwise there would have been a hurried slamming on of brakes, rapid swerving and a few unsavoury expletives.

Mr Hi-Vis was indifferent to all the excitement. He'd adopted the strategy of simply vanishing.

Expect the unexpected in a Devon lane... a (live, non-ghostly!) sheep walking along the top of a hedge: or maybe you'll meet a ghost wearing a hi-vis jacket?

BY TRAIN

Further along the A377 opposite The Rising Sun pub is Umberleigh railway station. Non-rural visitors often do not believe that this is a request stop.

A bridge goes over the track at the station taking the B3227 to South Molton. On several occasions, an elderly man wearing a cap and accompanied by a small dog, has been noticed crossing the bridge of an evening. Nothing unusual about a man taking his dog for a walk, except all reports tell of him disappearing before he reaches the end of the humped bridge. Where does he go? The parapet is not easy to climb over, and the drop down onto the railway track would be fatal. Kathy has frequently seen the old man walking his dog and has assumed him to be a present-day gentleman. It was only when I mentioned this particular chap that she realised he always disappears, and people she had been with hadn't seen him.

The road bridge over the track at Umberleigh Station

THE PORTSMOUTH ARMS, UMBERLEIGH

The Portsmouth Arms © *S. Anscombe*

How many old country pubs can boast their very own train station? The Portsmouth Arms at Umberleigh can, as the single-track Tarka Line running along the Taw Valley from Exeter St. David's to Barnstaple passes alongside this pub's back garden.

The pub itself is named for the fifth Earl of Portsmouth who inherited the nearby Eggesford estate. When the railway was built in 1854 the line encroached upon the earl's land, so he negotiated for a station to be built and trains to stop whenever he, or his guests, requested. But don't count on trains stopping so conveniently now, as the agreement has long since ceased, and the station is only an occasional request stop.

Originally the pub was built in 1420 as a toll house on the turnpike road between Barnstaple and Exeter, and was possibly once noted as a brothel. It is known that a woman died while at the bar: she keeled over and died with the suspicion of poisoning resulting in an autopsy. Fortunately for the pub's reputation, it proved that her death was by natural causes – not the beer!

Until Spring 2024, Steve Anscombe was the landlord for several years. One evening Kathy and I talked to him about some of his 'other' customers. He told us that he'd seen several presences, one had visited a few times and seemed to loiter near the dartboard. This figure had appeared from nowhere then disappeared through the back wall. Steve originally assumed the man was a policeman because of his smart uniform, cape and a cap. However, I pointed out that this sounded more like a railwayman's attire.

In the 1900s, before Dr Beeching recommended altering the twin line to a single track, a signal box had been situated alongside the station which was often busy with transporting livestock, milk, wool and agricultural goods. There was, therefore, a resident signalman *and* a station master, so the spirit near the dartboard could be either of these men. Both would have worn such a uniform.

A lady, thought to be named Emma or Emily, is also resident. She is dressed in white or cream, with what may be a 'bum roll' bustle beneath her gown – sausage-shaped padding to enhance the shape of the hips. Therefore, possibly the Queen Anne period or early Georgian. She has been seen near the present bar area and standing at one of the first-floor windows. Kathy has also seen a boy, dressed in Victorian or Edwardian style.

"Apart from the occasional inexplicable slamming of doors, none of the ghosts were a nuisance," Steve said. He left the pub in April 2024. The new management are most welcoming, friendly people with several ideas for hosting entertaining events offering locals and visitors an exciting future to blend with the remnants of the past?

An *old photograph of The Portsmouth Arms* © *The Portsmouth Arms*

HEAD BRIDGE

From the A377, take the B3226 towards King's Nympton and Chittlehamholt. The road crosses the River Mole at Head Bridge. The fields near the bridge are bordered by wooden fencing but be careful if driving along here: a man jumps over the fence and runs straight across the road. He vanishes before he reaches the other side. Was he running to or from something? There is no clear sighting of his style of dress, so no clue as to when he lived. A conundrum waiting to be solved?

There are several anecdotal reports of ghosts being seen in and around various hotels and pubs in the area, but the owners or managers did not want to be mentioned. It is a shame, but not everyone welcomes the presence of the paranormal – even when visitors are friendly.

CHAPTER 6
FURTHER AFIELD. NORTH DEVON – INLAND

SOUTH MOLTON

As with many Devon towns and villages, the market town of South Molton, which gained wealth from the wool trade, had its origins in the Anglo-Saxon era. It is mentioned in the Domesday Book: '*The king has one estate which is called South Molton* [modern spelling] *which King Eadweard held on the day that he himself was alive and dead.*' The last refers to the day King Edward, later known as The Confessor, died. (5th/6th January 1066.) As king's land, the estate would have passed to his successor, Harold II, but many references to Harold as King were deliberately obliterated by the Normans after 1066.

*'Harquebusier Trooper – King's Army, 1644', reproduced by
kind permission, © Chris Collingwood, historical artist*

During Oliver Cromwell's Interregnum following the English Civil War, the Sealed Knot, then a secretive organisation, now also a modern re-enactment society, was formed with the intention of overthrowing Cromwell and placing King Charles II on his rightful throne. They planned an uprising for the spring of 1655 but it was a failure. Following a small initial success in Salisbury, however, Sir John Penruddock headed west, and on 14th March his troop of exhausted men arrived at South Molton. Fierce fighting, which lasted for three hours, broke out in the streets between them and Cromwell's billeted Roundheads, resulting in Penruddock being captured and later beheaded at Exeter.

Defeated, the Royalists who survived fled. Some of the men who were captured were immediately executed, while seventy were sold into slavery and transported to the West Indies. It is not widely understood that many English, Scots and Irish men, women and children, suffered this fate under Cromwell's rule. It was only towards the latter half of the 1600s that black Africans were enslaved in their thousands, replacing the white Europeans who did not fare well in the colonial heat.

Only remnants of these armies, a couple of the South Molton soldiers – from either side – have been glimpsed. I am sure that more are there, but sadly, for various reasons, many modern-day people are reluctant to publicly speak about their encounters with spirits from the past.

South Molton, Broad Street, where you will find the Pannier Market and the Museum. Maybe a ghost or two?

A thriving market town, the majority of present-day buildings in South Molton date from the affluent Georgian era, including the Guildhall, which was completed in 1743 and is now the Town Hall, while beneath the old Assembly Rooms is the entrance to the town's Pannier Market.

Do spirits inhabit any of these old places? Apart from a few of the pubs, South Molton seems to be a quiet town as far as ghosts are concerned, although some encounters have been mentioned. There have been a number of spirits associated with the old police station, at one time situated in East Street with two cells for holding miscreants. The cells are still there and are reputed to be haunted.

Levi [surname withheld] mentioned that three different

people have seen a dark-haired female in one of the flats in Broad Street, while a neighbour's daughter encountered a ghost's presence in the museum.

The museum itself is well worth a visit, for it has many fascinating artefacts connected to the history of South Molton and surrounding area. If you see the ghost as well, that would be a bonus.

A very small claim to fame for South Molton occurred in 1964 - for the filming of *A Hard Day's Night* starring the Beatles. The black and white part-comedy film is now thought of as a classic and mimics the real life of the group. The Beatles, co-star Wilfred Brambell, and the movie crew travelled by train along the assumed quiet areas of the West Country in order to shoot the opening sequences. Word got out, and by the time they arrived at South Molton station the platform was crowded with eager fans. Alas, it is no use searching for the visiting ghosts of John Lennon or George Harrison as the station no longer exists, and anyway, only Ringo Starr got off the train to do some filming of his own on his cine camera.

The station, despite local protest, was closed by Dr Beeching in 1966.

NORTH MOLTON

There is a story of several ghost soldiers huddled together beneath a group of trees near North Molton. They are reported as wearing sashes and carrying muskets, so are possibly more participants of the English Civil War. The most common musket at that time was the matchlock, a cheaper version than the flintlock. These matchlock muskets had a smooth bore muzzle and were fired with a slow burning cord or 'match' which set off the priming charge of fine gunpowder previously placed in the 'pan', via the 'touch hole'. This ignited the main charge in the barrel. A failed attempt, when the gunpowder flared up but did not fire a loaded bullet was referred to as a 'flash in the pan,' a phrase still used today to mean a small event that went wrong or failed to happen.

There does not seem to be any harm intended by these spirits who are resting beneath the trees. I suspect that they are totally unaware of our presence.

Many spirits seem to linger beside or beneath trees

CHARLES

This tiny village near South Molton is gathered around a cluster of lanes and the parish church of St John the Baptist, overlooking the Bray Valley. The church is thought to date back to the 15th century, except the tower was rebuilt in 1620, with the rest of the church extensively restored in 1881.

Now merged into the Parish of Brayford, this quiet corner of Devon has deep-rooted memories for author Elizabeth St.John, who now lives in California. She was born in Barnstaple and returned often to Exmoor as a child on holiday with her parents. She told me a tale of not one unnerving ghostly experience, but an encounter with this entire village: "We used to visit High Bray on the edge of Exmoor," she explained. "In the sixties, we stayed on a lovely bed and breakfast working farm. The owners were most welcoming, with homemade clotted cream, a white cat called Snowball, and the most wonderful stories of the history of the land around the farm. However, they always warned us not to visit Charles, the tiny hamlet across the valley, especially after dark, for it did not like strangers. One evening after supper, as a highly imaginative nine-year-old, I persuaded my father to take me there. We wound our way up a steep hill and drove slowly through the quiet village. Not one light was showing anywhere, even though dusk was starting to fall. My father parked by the church and we got out of the car. The only sounds were jackdaws settling to roost in the trees and a whistling wind. There was, however, a great, unsettling sense of watchfulness and rejection, so different from all the cosy North Devon villages that dot the rest of the valley. I distinctly remember my father (who was an extremely sensible and practical RAF Officer), taking my hand, hurrying me back to the car and driving off down the lane without a backward glance. When our hostess heard of our adventure she shook her head, and forbade us to go back again to what she called the 'Ghost Village', although I've never managed to discover any information about any actual ghosts."

Although Elizabeth's historical novels do not involve Devon, they recount the stories of her ancestors: extraordinary women whose intriguing kinship with

England's kings and queens bring an intimately unique perspective to the time of the English Civil War. Her novels are inspired by family archives, residences and her family's history from Wiltshire's Lydiard Park to the imposing Tower of London.

ALLER CROSS, THE A361 LINK ROAD

Aller Cross is near Quince Honey Farm, which if you are interested in bees is a recommended visit. The grounds, planted especially to attract bees, are a delight to walk around, the shop is stocked with everything bee-related (including honey, of course), and the restaurant serves good food. On our farm we regularly host hives owned by Quince Honey Farm, the bees being a treasured resource for pollination.

On the A361 North Devon link road, sadly notorious for fatal tragedies, a man has, according to several witnesses, been seen running along the road near the Aller Cross roundabout, heading up the hill towards Barnstaple. He suddenly disappears, despite previously being clearly seen by drivers and passengers.

This particular stretch of road, however, dates from 1988 when the link road was extended from the previous route, with the old road to South Molton being downgraded to the B3227. There does not seem to be much of a specific description of the 'Running Man'; how is he dressed, for instance? His clothing could give a clue to his identity, or at least the era he comes from. Does he pre-date 1988 and have nothing to do with the present road layout?

GREAT TORRINGTON

Officially known as Great Torrington, to distinguish it from the nearby villages of Little Torrington and Black Torrington, the town is more commonly referred to simply as Torrington. (Tor'nt'n in local dialect.)

There are two hills named Castle Hill, the main one being within Torrington itself. It was once a Norman and Mediaeval castle built on what was originally an Iron Age hill fort. The site, to the south of the town, is situated on the edge of a high, steep precipice overlooking the River Torridge, with spectacular views along the valley – essential as a lookout for the English Civil War troops.

Not surprisingly, given its tragic history, several encounters with ghosts have been made at or near Torrington where the disastrous English Civil War battle took place and ended when gunpowder destroyed the church, taking many lives.

Several Civil War troopers, both foot and cavalry, have been seen particularly on the town's outskirts where much of the initial skirmishing took place. At least two hotels have had guests reporting strange encounters, while three sightings have been claimed for Castle Hill itself. One is of a Civil War figure who, to this day, still patrols his assigned watch.

'Parliamentary Harquebusier Officer c 1645'. Wearing an orange cummerbund. Reproduced by kind permission © Chris Collingwood, historical artist

A problem with identifying whether a ghostly apparition from the English Civil War is a Royalist or Parliamentarian is that both sides wore similar clothing. There was no uniform as such and men wore what they already had or could acquire. The assumption that Royalists favoured long flowing hair, elaborate feathered hats and lots of lace, while the Parliamentarians preferred leather and short-cropped hair is a bit of a myth. Very little actual evidence of clothing has survived; what we do know is stylised by paintings, which are usually of the gentry or well known figures, not the common soldiers.

The two practical and hardwearing fabrics mainly used were felted wool with a fuzzed nap, or natural, plain linen.

Outer garments were rarely washed but brushed, their colour gradually changed by ingrained dirt. It is assumed that underwear ('linens') were washed when opportunity arose. Colours would also fade by exposure to sunlight, grime and rain: dull grey, muddy browns, or perhaps re-dyed reds, greens, yellows and blues. Belts were narrow and worn *over* a coat to hold a bag of essential or personal equipment. Wearing just a linen smock, shirt and breeches? Then your ghost is more likely to be a labourer or farmer.

Soldiers' coats were usually made in quantity, funded by the regiment's colonel, with no specific fit and with no regular style or colour. A doublet of wool or linen would be worn; inside at the waist were steel eyes on a linen strip, which matched with hooks on the breeches and were used like braces to keep the breeches up.

Breeches were also wool or linen, of the same limited colours, but not always matching a coat, with the style dictated by the wearer's place of origin or class. Usually styled as loose and baggy, or closer fitting with less fabric around the seat area. Pockets would be leather or linen bags sewn into the side seams at the hip. Shoes were the same – no left and rights. Long boots were originally made for mounted cavalrymen. Woollen hose (stockings) came to the knee and were tied with a garter.

One way to tell the difference though: Royalist officers often wore rose-red sashes or cummerbunds, Parliamentarians wore tawny orange. These were silk items wound around the waist or over the shoulder, usually right to left and were large enough to double as a makeshift 'stretcher' to carry an injured man from the field 'hammock wise', a usage that continued regimentally for several centuries.

TORRINGTON STATION

Though the station was closed to passengers by Dr Beeching in 1965, freight trains continued to run from Torrington, hauling china clay and milk train traffic to London's Clapham Junction until 1982.

The station building was converted to a pub and then a café, and the railway line now forms part of the Tarka Trail cycle path network. In 2008, The Tarka Valley Railway Preservation Society was formed, with a short section of track and some rolling stock being preserved. In 2023, the society's first train ran along a 300-yard section of track, and long-term projects hope for an extension to become a tourist attraction. For now, though, if you are fortunate enough to see them, a stationmaster and his wife, dressed in what is believed to be pre-First World War attire, remain at the station and continue to follow their 1900s duties.

One other occurrence is my own when I experienced a detailed dream of a green-liveried locomotive pulling into a station too fast. I heard the brakes squealing and a gasp from the waiting passengers; felt the *whoosh* of the engine as it hurtled past. I had the feeling of being smaller than the people around me, as if I were a child. I clearly saw the locomotive's name and number as it swept past, 34031 *Torrington*. A *very* vivid dream.

I woke almost immediately and made a note of the number. On further investigation I discovered that this was a West Country Class, withdrawn from service in 1965 and existing now only as a Hornby model. But I had never heard of *Torrington* as a railway locomotive, nor had I any inkling of its number.

A dream or a supernatural memory? I wonder if this was a past-life encounter, which might explain why I am fascinated by steam locomotives. I am indebted to Mr Robert Jeffries for supplying a copyright-free image of *Torrington*, exactly as I saw her, although my view was in colour not black and white.

34031 Torrington. Original photograph reproduced by kind permission © Robert Jeffries

CHAPTER 7
VENTURING ONTO EXMOOR

The lonely moor where R.D. Blackmore set his novel, *Lorna Doone*, is spread along the north coast of Devon and Somerset, offering spectacular scenery. I have a few of my *Sea Witch Voyages* set on Exmoor, which include encounters with the Doone's fictional descendants. The wild landscape lends itself to my adventurous tales of 1700s derring-do.

Exmoor is where you might see the magnificent Red Deer roaming wild alongside herds of Exmoor ponies, distinctive by their 'mealy' or light-coloured muzzles. Thought to have ranged the Moor for several thousand years the breed almost went extinct towards the end of the 1900s, but careful management and breeding has, for now, saved these wonderful, highly intelligent ponies. Strictly speaking, they are not 'wild' but are owned by local landowners, each having their own registered herd name. The annual round-up in the autumn where the ponies are checked for their well-being before being released to roam freely again, is a sight to behold. At the time of writing this (winter 2024) we have four Exmoors, all were born on the Moor as ponies from the Farleywater herd.

The Exmoor Pony – our Mister Mischief, or 'Squidgy' who came from the Farleywater Herd as a two-year-old. He is now in his twenties

TARR STEPS

The devil is said to have built Tarr Steps, an ancient clapper bridge and scheduled monument, consisting of seventeen huge stone slabs weighing about two tons each. No mortar or cement has been used. The bridge is thought to be the oldest and longest (fifty-five yards) of its kind in the UK, possibly dating back hundreds, if not thousands, of years. In Medieval Latin *claperius* means 'pile of stones'.

According to legend the devil built the bridge for his own use, but a local parson negotiated a deal for the villagers to cross it when the devil wasn't in need of it. A pity the devil didn't make some sort of different arrangement for, despite their weight, the stones have been washed away several times during flood storms, but thankfully, always restored. The winter of 1941-1942 saw the middle section damaged, and more was sustained in 2012, 2016 and 2017. Steel cables are now positioned upriver to help reduce storm debris reaching the bridge.

As for ghosts, you are not likely to meet the devil, unless you are very unlucky. You might, however, notice a cat keeping his paws dry by making use of the bridge - but he (or she?) disappears halfway across.

The Devil's Bridge, Tarr Steps © Tony Smith

THE VALLEY OF THE ROCKS

The devil appears to have been busy on Exmoor, for it is also said that he built a castle overlooking the sea but, betrayed by the mistresses he kept there, in a fit of temper he destroyed the building, and all that is left are the remaining rocks. An amusing tale to explain the natural formation of the

Valley of the Rocks, thought to have been formed during the Ice Age.

There is a tentative report of a ghost Exmoor pony and her foal seen cantering away from this iconic rock formation. They might have been real ponies, but they inexplicably disappeared and on inspection, although the ground was exceptionally muddy, there was no sign of any hoofprints.

With the valley also inhabited by feral goats, there are, apparently, no human ghosts lingering in the area. Perhaps they don't like the goats?

The Devil's Castle - Valley of the Rocks © Cathy Helms

THE LONELY MOOR

A huntsman riding across Exmoor has been noticed on several occasions by different people. All report the same: he appears from nowhere, rides a short distance, then disappears again.

Pixies are said to roam Exmoor with many place names

relating to them: Pixie Copse, Pixie Meadow, Pixie Lane and Pixie Rocks. They are tiny, quick, fairy folk who live in small turf-covered dwellings built in crevices and well hidden secretive places. Traditional legend states that the King of the Pixies lived near Withypool, with nearby farmers being helped by the pixies with the threshing of corn in return for the gift of milk left out for them at night.

One very active anomaly on the moor was said to be Jack O'Lantern who appeared as a wraith-like blue mist, seen by many Exmoor travellers who believed that he was trying to lure them into hidden bogs. Was he a ghostly spirit or a mischievous pixie? The blue colour gives the game away. Methane gas used to ooze from the boggy moorland, appearing as if it was a moving supernatural creature. But 'Jack' has not been seen since extensive moorland drainage was undertaken during the late 19th and early 20th centuries, which dispersed the gassy deposits.

With the environmental re-wetting programmes now in place to counter climate change, will the methane return along with the will o'the wisp, Jack O'Lantern?

OARE

Also associated with *Lorna Doone*, Oare and the Doone Valley is a popular tourist spot, but beware of the ghost of a witch who might be sighted after dark beside a holly tree that grows beside a gateway just outside of the village. She is said to be small so she could even be an Exmoor pixie. She seems harmless, however, so if you do spot her, nod a greeting and walk on by.

Reports of pistol shots and wild cries borne on the wind have been mentioned in the same area, with fearsome men riding across the moor sometimes being sighted. The outlaw clan of the Doones perhaps, although Blackmore did make them up as fictional characters. The tales of ghost riders were probably invented and spread by the prolific smuggling gangs in order to keep snooping Excise Men off the moor. Or maybe a real ghost or two inspired the stories in the first place?

THE STAGHUNTERS INN, BRENDON

The Staghunters Inn, Brendon, Exmoor

An afternoon drive onto Exmoor took Kathy and me to this friendly old inn, owned and run by members of the Wyburn family. Originally, the site had been the location of an abbey before the dissolution of the monasteries by Henry VIII c.1536. The chapel is the only part to survive.

VENTURING ONTO EXMOOR

One of the comfortable (haunted?) bedrooms at the Staghunters Inn

Simon Wyburn told us that he has always been interested in the supernatural. "Customers," he said with an enthusiastic smile, "have reported seeing a monk, and upstairs there is a woman who lingers in one of the bedrooms, while unexplained footsteps are regularly heard outside the rooms. I have also seen a large, glowing orb of light along the corridor downstairs. A lady with long hair and a long dress has been seen clearly, or as a misty apparition, in the public area of the inn: she walks through a wall where there used to be a door, and heads towards the river where she disappears." He added that orbs have appeared in photographs.

Kathy was delighted to tell him that while he was talking

to us, she could see a monk standing behind the bar. "He is dressed in a grey robe with a hood and a white rope belt around his waist." She could smell musty herbs on the floor, while out the back of the pub she encountered two more monks, similarly dressed, tending a herb garden. Another monk stood at the far end of the chapel.

Simon Wyburn welcomes all visitors to The Staghunters Inn © The Staghunters Inn

Kathy noticed a distinct 'presence' in the restaurant and lounge area. "I think this was the lady who has been seen to walk through the wall," she said. "For some reason the lady was reluctant to reveal herself to me."

VENTURING ONTO EXMOOR

Even if there are ghostly spirits wandering around, The Staghunters Inn has a relaxed and welcoming atmosphere

The monks Kathy saw all wore grey robes, varying from a light colour to darker charcoal. This, along with the knotted rope belts might indicate that they were Franciscans. The only puzzle, if so, is that the original building would have been a *friary*, not an *abbey* – but it is a long time since the 16th century, maybe the status of a derelict religious building became misinterpreted in later years?

Also outside, Kathy could smell horses, (there were none there) in what used to be the stables. The monks and the other spirits Kathy became aware of were all friendly, giving no sense of fear or hostility, so if you are visiting Exmoor, do enjoy a drink, meal or even a holiday stay at this lovely old inn.

SIMONSBATH (SAY IT 'SIMMONSBATH')

Exmoor was extensively used as a training ground for Second World War troops, where sadly much of the wildlife suffered, including the Red Deer and the Exmoor ponies, slaughtered as meat to augment insufficient rations. During one military operation in the winter of 1940 every road in the area of Simonsbath became blocked by troop transport. Heavy rain and sleet turned into a blizzard that lasted for an entire day and night, adding to the gridlock. As the snow formed, huge drifts of three or four feet mounted up. Men abandoned their equipment to seek shelter from the appalling weather.

Most were lucky and survived the bitter cold, but at least seven died. Are theirs the spirits that have been seen roaming the moor in this area?

LYNTON AND LYNMOUTH

Lynton and Lynmouth, connected by a funicular railway, rose to fame during the Victorian period when fern collecting became a popular hobby, deemed respectable, even for women. The ladies enjoyed scrabbling around the steep sides of the scenic gorge, identifying and gathering the many different types of ferns. The familiar pattern on Custard Cream biscuits is said to have derived from this botanic interest.

In 1952 Lynton and Lynmouth hit the headlines when a devastating flood killed thirty-five people and made 420 homeless. Do any of their spirits remain? Several hotels claim pale figures of ladies standing anxiously over guests' beds, while a black-clad monk haunted the Lynton estate because he was refused entry to the old castle. As he does not seem to have been spotted for some years now, he has presumably forgiven the insult and moved on.

More than forty-five ghosts are said to reside in a hot spot area near Sinai House. A tree near there was used to hang felons and witches, leaving a disturbing presence from distressed souls which may affect today's passers-by. Monks, soldiers, weeping women and other apparitions, some benign, some hostile, regularly appear in the vicinity.

Contrary to popular belief, witches in England were not burned alive. This horrendous punishment was reserved for traitors and heretics. Witches were more usually hanged. Devon has several tales of witch hunts and trials; the best known is connected to Bideford – discover more later!

You might also notice a woman wandering along the headland of Countisbury Hill. It is not known who she is or why she walks there. However, do not offer her a lift, as by the time you stop, she will have gone.

The lonely road near Countisbury Hill, Lynmouth © Cheryl Witcombe

CHAPTER 8
FURTHER DOWN THE COAST

COMBE MARTIN

George Ley of Combe Martin enjoyed a game of cards and in 1690, after a satisfying win, he built a house to reflect his passion. Named as The Pack O' Cards, the building has four floors for the four suits, with thirteen rooms representing the number of cards in a suit. There are fifty-two windows and fifty-two stairs.

There does not, however, seem to be fifty-two ghosts, but there are at least four of them in this quirky old place; a small, bearded man is said to roam around the floors, while two ghosts remain hiding from the Press Gang who came searching for new Royal Navy recruits. The fourth ghost is a woman wearing a long white, flowing gown.

At Combe Martin church, a procession of priests led by a bishop and followed by the parish men and women walk through the church in silence before – yes, you guessed: disappearing.

ILFRACOMBE

It is not always pubs or historic buildings that have ghostly guests. A young Ilfracombe mum and dad told me of, "A lady dressed in an old-fashioned style, peering with a smile into our baby's cot." Another time, they heard a voice coming over the baby monitor singing a gentle lullaby. The couple were sitting downstairs watching TV with no one else in the house. When Mum went up to investigate the baby was contentedly asleep. "We weren't worried," she said. "Free childminding is always welcome."

Ilfracombe Harbour with Verity standing proud against the sky
© *Cheryl Witcombe*

Loaned to the town for a period of twenty years, Verity is a stainless steel and bronze statue, either liked or loathed. Created by Ilfracombe resident, Damien Hirst and erected in 2012, she is a 66.4ft sculpture on the pier at the entrance to Ilfracombe harbour. Verity depicts justice, 'Verity' as a name, meaning truth.

She is a heavily pregnant woman holding high a sword in one hand, with the scales of justice in the other while straddled atop a pile of law books. What makes the sculpture controversial is that half of her shows her internal anatomy, including the foetus. Kathy and I think she is magnificent.

Opposite Verity, on the other side of the narrow channel is a sheltered beach, Rapparee Cove. When the tide is favourable, visitors can enjoy a pleasant morning or afternoon there, but reports of uneasiness have been mentioned, along with several children disliking the place. There appears to be a lingering presence from a 1796 shipwreck which took several lives during a storm.

THE GEORGE AND DRAGON

A popular pub for ghost tour events, The George and Dragon boasts over fifty different spirits – of the paranormal kind, not bottles behind the bar. Many seem to be dock workers or sailors, for Ilfracombe was once a busy harbour town.

As a non-nautical visitor, an elderly lady is frequently observed. She wears a hat and is either waiting to be served at the bar, or sits in a corner near the fire. Visitors have moved aside to let her pass, then wondered where she went. There is an old photograph hanging on the wall depicting a woman who died many years ago. Customers declare that they have seen the same lady sitting in the pub.

MORTEHOE

Perched above Exmoor's cliffs is the village of Mortehoe. The name is a giveaway as *Morte* is French for death, and the dangerous rocks along this coast are adequate explanation. Mortehoe Museum is interesting, as is a walk along the South

West Coast Path offering spectacular views and an abundance of wildlife.

The village is rich in architecture, especially the 13th-century barrel-roofed St. Mary's Church, but as for ghosts, many a sailor met his doom on those jagged rocks and legends abound of smugglers and wreckers. But smugglers are more likely to have used easier beaches to bring their contraband ashore, while, despite the myths there are no records of anyone being accused of, or arrested for, using lights to lure ships onto rocks. Any sailors worth their salt seeing lights would, in fact, steer in the *opposite* direction further out to sea, so *deliberate* wrecking is more likely to be Victorian Fake News.

However, this *is* a dangerous stretch of water and many a tall ship ran aground during storms. It was not illegal to salvage any cargo that floated ashore from a shipwreck. Sadly, such were the times that salvaging goods took priority over saving lives. Many a ghost must roam this coast, resenting the fact that life was not regarded as more precious than the cargo a ship carried.

One ghost in particular was not a sailor. Sir William de Tracey was one of the men who murdered Thomas à Beckett in Canterbury Cathedral in 1170. After the deed he fled Kent and in self-imposed exile, spent what remained of his life wandering along the beach between Ilfracombe and Mortehoe, his daughter secretly taking him food. When he died his spirit remained, wandering up and down, forever penitent.

WOOLACOMBE

A woman, dressed in the inevitable white, has been observed walking along the beach at Woolacombe, apparently unperturbed by deep pools of water or other hazards that she encounters by simply walking *through* them – including large rocks. A young girl has been seen by several different people near the holiday park, although her shape is indistinct and often quite misty.

Barricane Beach, Woolacombe © Hazel Bowles

BRAUNTON BURROWS, SAUNTON SANDS AND LUNDY ISLAND

Braunton village is five miles west of Barnstaple, and nearby, facing the edge of the wild Atlantic Ocean, is Braunton

Burrows which forms one of the largest sand dune systems in England. The adjoining Saunton Sands, with its three miles of sandy beach is a fabulous place for surfing or dabbling in rock pools.

Jack White Hat paces the shore at Braunton Burrows calling for the Appledore and Instow ferryman to come and collect him, or begs anyone with a boat to take him across. Upon agreement to do so, Jack vanishes. A harmless, but troubled soul.

I have set some of my nautical *Sea Witch Voyages* near Crow Point, an area where fiction and supernatural beings and events, as well as historical shipwrecks, fire the imagination. Evocative places and old legends are a treat for fiction authors.

Crow Point, Braunton Burrows. An ideal setting for smugglers, pirates and fiction writers © Alison and Paul Sopp

On a clear day Lundy Island can be seen. Famous for its colony of puffins, Lundy is bursting with the history of pirates and smugglers. There are one or two ghosts, sailors lingering from tragic shipwrecks, but one wreck was deliberately masterminded in 1752 by Appledore dignitary and resident, Thomas Benson. Unable to pay owed taxes, he organised the sinking of his ship, *Nightingale* in an attempt to claim the insurance for the ship and its cargo. The plan failed, the captain paid the penalty by being hanged for fraud, while Benson fled to Portugal. I use the young Tom Benson as a character in my *Sea Witch Voyages* series.

Saunton Sands with Lundy Island on the horizon. According to local tradition: if you can't see Lundy it's raining. If you can see it – it's about to rain!

ARLINGTON COURT

Just off the A39 is Arlington Court, a beautiful old house and carriage museum, with lakes, woods and gardens to explore. Home to several generations of the Chichester family for over 150 years, the original house, built in 1820-23, replaced an earlier, now demolished, country estate. Last in line, unmarried Rosalie Chichester was an independent woman and a talented artist with an interest in flora and fauna. She donated the house and land to the National Trust in 1947, two years before she died aged 85. Her ashes are interred in a commemorative urn set at her favourite spot beside the lake. There have been several sightings here of a young woman in her early twenties wearing a blue dress. People who have seen this serene lady have stated that she bears a striking resemblance to photographs of Miss Chichester that are displayed in the house.

If visiting Arlington Court, don't miss the nearby St James' church, which replaced an earlier building and dates to around the late 1600s. One early remnant is the effigy of Thomasine Raleigh, set into a niche in the north wall of the chancel. She is thought to be one of the De Raleigh family who owned the manor before it passed to the Chichesters in 1365. A Catholic priest, carrying a lantern, has also been seen on several occasions near the church porch.

Arlington Court, St James' Church © Tony Smith

CHAPTER 9
BARNSTAPLE

For an old town Barnstaple itself does not seem to host many active ghosts. Maybe they like to keep themselves to themselves, or perhaps people are reluctant to talk about their encountered experiences?

The Anglo-Saxons were early settlers, although I'm sure that the Romans made use of the River Taw, and would have had a fortress and trade settlement of some sort near what is now the Old Bridge, the river's lowest, safe, crossing point before reaching the Bristol Channel at Instow and Appledore. Perhaps there are Roman foundations beneath the Georgian buildings?

The wool trade created the town's wealth from the 14th century until the 18th, when the river silted up. Allegedly founded by the Saxon, King Alfred the Great, Barnstaple was one of the first towns outside of York and London to have its own mint prior to the Norman Conquest. There are a few known ghosts to augment its history…

BARNSTAPLE CASTLE

Situated in the corner of the Tuly Street carpark, next to Barnstaple Library, this ancient shell-keep is not a castle as we are familiar with, as this is all that remains of a Motte and Bailey Norman fortification built some time between 1070-1120. If the earlier date, then possibly on the orders of the victor of the Battle of Hastings in 1066 – Duke William of Normandy.

Built over a Saxon cemetery, the fortification would have commanded a strategic view over the river and town. Stone buildings and defences replaced the original wooden palisade fence and inner keep during the 1100s, with Henry III later ordering the Sheriff of Devon to ensure that the walls did not exceed ten feet in height. By 1274 it was beginning to crumble into decay, and by 1326 was a ruin, with the stonework removed and used elsewhere. The final existing section was recorded by John Leland in an itinerary published in 1542, where he mentions some dungeons remaining to the north-west of Barnstaple near the bridge. The last of the derelict castle walls collapsed during a storm in 1601.

Except... some residents from the past are still there. Stand near the library and glance up to the top of the mound; you might see three Norman soldiers aiming crossbows at you.

The remains of the Norman Motte and Bailey castle, Barnstaple

THE PANNIER MARKET

Pannier markets are distinctive to the West Country, 'pannier' coming from the French 'basket', referring to goods brought to market in baskets on the backs of pack animals. Barnstaple's Pannier Market was built in the mid-1800s and is an excellent example of this type of indoor marketplace. Recently renovated to a high standard by North Devon Council it is, with or without the attraction of any spirits or ghosts, a good place to shop or browse. The first official market in Barnstaple was recorded in 1274 and by the 14th century the town was

Devon's third richest after Exeter and Plymouth. In 1588 five ships funded by Barnstaple were despatched to aid against the attempted invasion by the Spanish Armada.

During the Stuart age, trade increased with the expansion of the tobacco industry from Virginia and the Colonies. Wealthy merchants built their grand houses and a few of these survive, though many have Georgian renovations.

Barnstaple's river was already slowly silting up. Bideford, with the faster-flowing Torridge took over the water trade during the late 1680s, and by 1730 it had become the main port of call for deeper-draft ocean-going ships. Barnstaple's low-draft trade continued well into the 20th century, and today the town is a popular place to visit – and a location for ghost tours and stories.

The newly refurbished Barnstaple Pannier Market from Butcher's Row

ST ANNE'S

A 14th-century chapel, St Anne's is between Boutport Street and the pannier market and is Barnstaple's only surviving Chantry Chapel, which were places where a mass was regularly held for the souls of the departed. St Anne's ceased to be a religious building *c.*1650 but in 1685 Huguenot refugees, escaping French religious tyranny, found their way to Barnstaple and were given permission to use the chapel as a meeting house when it was not required as a school. This arrangement continued until 1910. The place then became a museum, but was abandoned in 1997. Fortunately, it has been restored and is now an art and community centre, and the rendezvous for some excellent ghost tours.

St Anne's has an interesting undercroft, once used as a charnel house where disturbed bones from the overcrowded graveyard outside were stored. This grassy area still has several gravestones that have fallen or been moved, but it is believed that the remains of about 1,500 people were laid to rest here, all one atop the other with the upper layer only six inches below the present surface.

In 1909 the rumour of a ghostly sighting at St Anne's spread rapidly through the town. One man subsequently claimed that he had photographed a misty apparition rising from one of the graves. He displayed the photo in his window, but unfortunately the photograph no longer exists – it mysteriously went missing. Nor is it known who the man was.

Not that it matters. The photograph, as with the Cottingley Fairies, was probably a clever fake.

St Anne's Chapel, Barnstaple

BOUTPORT STREET

Until 1869 a licence, obtained from a magistrate, was needed to run a fully licensed pub or inn, while smaller beerhouses did not require official status as they paid a fee to trade to the Excise Department. Beerhouses often did not last long, and were usually known as tiddlywink or kiddlywink bars. By 1837 there were eighty-one fully licensed premises in Barnstaple.

One was The Bull Inn, situated on Boutport Street, one of Barnstaple's oldest streets, although the pub occasionally went under different names. It is mentioned in R.D. Blackmore's *Lorna Doone* as the inn where highwayman Tom Faggus regularly visited. The pub is now long gone, replaced by the modern Green Lanes shopping centre, but the story of a ghost lingers...

Bob, a regular at the pub, lost a leg in the second world war, the landlady could hear the tapping of his crutch approaching so always had a pint ready and waiting for him. Bob preferred to sit in the same chair by the door, and when he died the landlady and many customers went to his funeral. Some days later, the landlady heard the familiar tap-tap-tapping and automatically drew the usual pint. The door opened, the tapping continued, and the chair scraped on the floor...

"Evenin' Bob," she called out, and heard his customary answer, "Evenin' maid!" And then she realised that Bob had been buried several days previously.

Boutport Street, where Georgian buildings rank alongside the modern Green Lanes shopping centre – and the occasional ghost waits for a bus

A BUS RIDE FROM GREEN LANES TO NORTH DEVON HOSPITAL

With only one passenger already aboard, a bus driver stopped at the Green Lanes shopping centre to pick up an elderly lady and a younger man who carried a bunch of carnations and wore a leather jacket. The man already had a ticket, but issuing the lady with an O.A.P concessionary ticket, the driver enquired whether they were going to the hospital, but received no answer. The two sat next to each other. At the hospital – the next stop – only the original passenger got off, there was no sign of the other two. The concessionary ticket that the driver had issued was still in the machine.

Other bus drivers have told of smelling fresh cigar smoke on an empty bus, and hearing the bell ringing on a bus that was out of service.

THE CINEMA AND GUILDHALL

The ghost of a former employee wanders around in Barnstaple's cinema. He died in 1931 while repairing the roof, but has stayed, occasionally showing himself. I wonder if he has a favourite genre of film that he particularly likes to watch?

Staff at the nearby Guildhall have reported seeing two deceased council members strolling through the council offices long after normal working hours.

CHAPTER 10
BEYOND BARNSTAPLE

TAWSTOCK COURT

Tawstock Court was once an important North Devon manor. The original site has a long history, and was a residence of successive families – de Totnes, de Braose, Audley and several more. St Peter's church, nearby, was built in the 12th century, added to in the 14th and restored between 1867-1868. The only part that remains of the once grand Elizabethan mansion which replaced the original Norman manor, is the gatehouse, built in 1574. The house itself was destroyed by fire in 1787 and rebuilt in a neo-gothic style c.1800. After being used as a school for many years, the property was sold to a private investor in 2012.

Several tales of ghosts exist. An elderly lady walks across the lawn, a stick in her hand and a heavy basket upon her back. Carrying collected firewood perhaps, or acorns, hazel and beechnuts to feed her pigs?

A hooded monk can be seen walking straight through a gravestone before entering the church.

Tawstock Court and St Peter's Church, where an elderly lady walks across the lawns gathering firewood maybe?

INSTOW

The small town of Instow is opposite Appledore where the two rivers of the Taw and Torridge form an estuary which, until it silted up, was busy with shipping, both for trade and ship building.

For keen walkers or cyclists, the Tarka Trail passes through Instow, and the old railway tunnel can claim some spooky food for the imagination, but it must be borne in mind that old tunnels carry modern noises, especially from mobile phone or radio signals, so any 'ghostly voices' are nothing more than stray eavesdropping.

The old quayside and small beach at Instow has good views across the estuary towards Appledore, and a couple of the Instow premises boast encounters with former residents. One in particular has a young lady who likes to keep guests from enjoying a good sleep by sitting on the bed. Ghostly cricketers have been seen by a few dog-walkers, playing a lively game near the beach. "Out for a ghost" instead of "out for a duck" – a cricketing term which means bowled out, or dismissed, before getting any runs.

Instow from Appledore © Cathy Helms

Appledore from Instow © Simon Murgatroyd

APPLEDORE AND NORTHAM

Today, Appledore is a picturesque village with narrow cobbled streets and alleyways known as 'opes', nestling on a steep hillside beside the estuary confluence of the rivers Taw and Torridge.

An Appledore 'ope'

Appledore began to prosper during the reign of Elizabeth I due to increasing trade with the North American colonies, while Bideford, a few miles up the River Torridge, rapidly became the third largest English trade port for Virginia tobacco. With its rich maritime history and quaint cottages, Appledore is a must to visit, particularly during September when the Appledore Literary Festival is in full swing. For our interest, though, we need to travel further back in time.

Appledore Book Festival 2023 © Annie Whitehead, participating author, seated centre

Originally an Anglo-Saxon settlement, Appledore is the possible site of two important battles, one involving Viking raiders in 878 CE and another a rebellion that, had it been successful, could have altered English history.

On certain nights it is said that near the shore, fierce fighting can be heard and the flickering shadows of men can be observed. However, even though there is a memorial stone to a Viking raid in the wall at Bloody Corner in Northam, this story may be nothing more than a legend. During the time of Alfred the Great, Hubba the Dane – or more likely the name should be Ubba – landed at Boathyde with a fleet of ships and was soundly defeated, losing over 1,000 men.

The memorial reads:

> *"Stop Stranger Stop,*
> *Near this spot lies buried*
> *King Hubba the Dane,*
> *who was slayed in a bloody retreat,*
> *by King Alfred the Great"*

Hubba/Ubba was slain *somewhere* in the West Country, although there is no evidence to support Appledore as the location, *but...* there is possible evidence that the sons of King Harold II, slain at the Battle of Hastings in 1066, attempted a rebellion here, which unfortunately failed.

> '*After this came Harold's sons from Ireland, at Midsummer, with 64 ships into the mouth of the Taw, and there heedlessly landed; and Earl Brian [Brian of Brittany] came against them unawares with no small band, and fought against them.*' [*Anglo–Saxon Chronicle, Manuscript D.*]

This is plausible. King Harold II's mother, Gytha, owned extensive land in North Devon during the 11th century. Harold himself landed at Porlock after a short exile to Ireland in 1052/3, and it is inconceivable that his sons and supporters did not attempt to defeat Duke William after the tragedy of October 14th 1066. The entry in the *Anglo-Saxon Chronicle* mentions the mouth of the River Taw, so Appledore would certainly fit the bill in terms of location and so perhaps it really was here that the fighting took place, although, sadly, Harold's sons were defeated and could not avenge their father's death.

Unfortunately no one seems to have *seen* any desperate English fyrdsmen fighting for *Englalond*. But Kathy and I are sure they are there. Are these the *sounds* of Harold's sons and their men that have been heard on many occasions?

Nearer our time, there are many sightings of sailors and fishermen reported by residents and visitors to Appledore and Bideford. The ghost of an early 1900s Frenchman is occasionally seen and heard, claiming to be the murdered victim of inhospitable residents, although documented records point to him being slain by one of his fellow sailors.

A boy in early Georgian clothing has been seen on the beach at low tide, jumping over the thick cable of an anchored tall ship, while ghost ships have been seen tackling the dangerous currents just inside the sandbar where the rivers become the sea. Along the road approaching Appledore, a horse and cart, carrying a well-dressed man and a young boy, has been seen plodding along before suddenly disappearing.

The narrow streets of old Appledore

HARTLAND

Ghostly lights have been reported on the windswept headland of Hartland, along with two headless ladies who walk around in silk dresses. A monk clad in black ambles around the church, while a group of Brothers walk from the church in the direction of the former abbey.

The presence of a teenage girl remains in the area. She is said to be named Elvira, who was murdered by a gypsy.

BIDEFORD

Mrs Bell, an Edwardian lady from a Bideford property, liked to play Chopin on her piano. Until recently she continued to do so, even though she had died in the early 1900s. She had been the custodian of an art collection, with one painting being a portrait of herself sitting at her beloved piano, but shortly before her death she had sold the collection because of bankruptcy. Distraught at the loss of her painting, Mrs Bell's ghost continued to look for it. Several people witnessed her apparition, wreathed by a bluish haze, wandering through the house accompanied by the sound of Chopin.

Then one day, the owner of the house was contacted by a local antique dealer who had a painting which turned out, after investigation, to be the portrait of Mrs Bell. This intriguing story was revealed on BBC TV when the owner took the painting to the *Antiques Roadshow* for evaluation. The portrait is now displayed in the drawing room of the house in question [private property], and Mrs Bell has not been seen since.

Strange noises and a definite presence were often reported by unauthorised teenage visitors to a derelict house which once formed the heart of Bideford Zoo. The zoo closed in the 1970s and the abandoned house was eventually restored to become private apartments – whether any lingering ghosts remain there is untold.

Author J.G. Harlond remembers a tale from her Bideford schooldays in 1966-68. A house in Cross Street called in a vicar to exorcise a poltergeist. No one remembered whether the vicar was successful though. The word 'poltergeist' comes from German *polter*, meaning noisy and *geist*, spirit.

Several Bideford residents in private homes tell of various

experiences of seeing strangers in addition to recently departed family members. Two people, in different houses, have spoken of smelling lavender. The ancient Egyptians used lavender as a perfume, and traces of it were found in Tutankhamun's tomb, the aroma still quite strong. The Romans are thought to have brought the plant to Britain as it was used as an antiseptic. Its benefits were also thought to ward off sickness, the plague – and restless spirits.

Bideford is also noted as being famous for the witch trials of 1682, the three victims are believed to be the last women to be executed for witchcraft in England.

Two other women were from well-to-do families and were acquitted, but the unfortunate three, Temperance Lloyd, Mary Trembles and Susanna Edwards, had no such advantage and were convicted. Temperance Lloyd came to Devon from Wales after the Civil War. She lived in poverty and sold apples to get by. A child stole an apple and some time later fell ill. Then shopkeeper Thomas Eastchurch's sister-in-law, Grace Thomas, also became ill. Master Eastchurch claimed that he had overheard Temperance admitting to knowing a mysterious stranger who had instructed her to kill Grace. The man was believed to be the devil. More Bideford people gave various witness statements about Temperance – statements that today would be dismissed firmly as superstitious or malevolent nonsense. However, Temperance was arrested and questioned, and eventually admitted to many misdeeds of witchcraft when moved to Exeter Gaol for trial.

A few weeks later, two further destitute women were accused. Mary Trembles was of Irish descent, unmarried and, on her own following the deaths of her parents, she resorted to begging. Susanna Edwards was born illegitimate and widowed young. She had been overheard telling of how the devil had intimately known her, and that she and Mary had been told to assist in harming Grace. Both confessed to using witchcraft.

All three were tried at Exeter, with the crime of witchcraft being enough to convict them. At this time imprisonment would have been the normal punishment, but executions were urged in case an uprising of riots and an increase of witchcraft would follow. The women were hanged in Exeter on 25th August 1682, with their bodies transferred to unconsecrated ground which is now within the car park at the University of Exeter. Their ghosts do not seem to haunt their traumatic experience in Exeter, but do they remain in Bideford, perhaps?

CLOVELLY

The cobbles of Clovelly © Alison and Paul Sopp

Privately owned by the Hamlyn family since 1738, Clovelly is managed by the Clovelly Estate Company, and with its steep, cobbled main street and traditional architecture it is one of North Devon's quaintest seaside villages. Donkeys were used to transport people and goods up and down the gradient, but these have been replaced by wooden sledges, often parked outside houses where in other villages there would be a car. To reach the village there is a fee to pay at the visitor centre which covers parking and entrance to the two museums.

Clovelly transport: most houses have their own sledge © Alison and Paul Sopp

Since the Iron Age people have lived nearby, with the Manor of Clovelly being acquired by Duke William of Normandy after 1066. Until the late 1600s the village was mainly farm orientated, until Squire George Cary took the initiative of having a stone breakwater erected to form a suitable fishing harbour, creating the only safe place for anchorage along this stretch of rugged coast. With the harbour came fish cellars and warehouses, while cottages were built alongside the stream that ran from the cliff top to the shore. Christine Hamlyn inherited the estate in 1884 and Clovelly owes much to her enthusiasm to renovate and preserve many of these cottages within what had become a dilapidated village.

Clovelly Court Gardens offer the chance to view beautiful gardens and restored Victorian greenhouses. One supernatural report is of an old gardener who is tucked away in a sunny corner quietly taking a secret snooze. He needn't worry about being caught out, though, as when spotted he instantly vanishes.

An 18th-century ghoulish story is associated with Clovelly, concerning a tribe of murderous cannibals. The fictional tale is of a gang who ambushed travellers, killed and ate them back at their cave hideaway. The story more likely stems from tales deliberately spread by smugglers in order to keep prying eyes away from their nocturnal activities. Several 'victims' haunt the coast to this day, but these are more likely to be the spirits of shipwrecked sailors.

Clovelly Harbour © Alison and Paul Sopp

A farm near Clovelly plays host to an English Civil War Royalist who walks through the wall of a room at the rear of the house, and a stay at the hotel near the quay might give the bonus of meeting one of their many resident ghosts.

One present-day visitor, who wishes to remain anonymous, related that he saw a young lady in 'old fashioned' clothing standing near the harbour, staring forlornly out to sea.

"The second time I saw her, I noticed that she was weeping, so I went to see if I could comfort her obvious distress, but as I approached she faded into a mist and disappeared." The poor woman is, perhaps, awaiting a sweetheart, husband or brother who went to sea and never returned.

WESTWARD HO!

There are very few places that can claim an exclamation mark in the title, or became established because of a story. Westward Ho! is one of those few and is named after the book by Charles Kingsley, which he published in 1855. The story itself is set in nearby Bideford and became a bestseller. Taking advantage of the wonderful beach, sea bathing and the healthy breeze, all great passions for the Victorians, visitors flocked to the area and a tourist centre and accommodation sprang up, which soon expanded into a thriving village.

Seafield House, built *c*.1885, has a reputation of being 'spooky' because it fell into disuse and rapidly became derelict. It has an air of a Victorian Gothic haunted house, a reputation increased by *Help! My House is Haunted*, when the TV team claimed they had made contact with several spirits. A fire a few days later was blamed on the ghosts being disgruntled at being disturbed. Another rumour is that a lady can be seen waving from an upstairs window. There isn't much credence to any of these tales, though, and one must be sceptical about the dramatic TV claims.

ABBOTSHAM, BUCKLAND BREWER AND 'WOOLSERY'.

A taxi driver waits for a customer who never arrives at the Old Thatched Inn, Abbotsham, and dogs frequently react to an invisible presence there. While just under five miles from Bideford is the village of Buckland Brewer and The Coach and Horses, where two cavaliers are said to linger in the corner of an upstairs room. Were they also connected to the disaster at Torrington, or is their continuing presence a memory of some other English Civil War skirmish? One man of the New Model Army – a Roundhead – has also been seen at this delightful old pub, which is rare, for king's men in ghost form seem more prolific than Oliver Cromwell's followers.

A woman dressed in black has also been observed by several different people within the pub but unfortunately, no detailed description has been shared.

Woolfardisworthy, along with a few other places in Devon is noted for one of the longest place names in England. More commonly, however, it is known as Woolsery. (Say it *Wulzery*.) The Farmers Arms there, has a spirit which either dislikes clocks or is angry about something, for he (or she) has been known to throw the clock across the kitchen, or hurls various items at the staff. Outside, the ghost of a man, possibly a vagrant, has been seen loitering beside the Anglo-Saxon well.

Maybe he is staying out of the way of the clock-thrower?

CHAPTER II
FOUR-FOOTED BEASTS

Several public houses have various animal pets that not everyone is aware of. A pub in Ilfracombe has a dog that brushes past customers' legs, The Exeter Inn, Chittlehamholt, has at least two ghost cats, one a white kitten, while The Portsmouth Arms, Umberleigh, has the distinction of being visited by a wild boar.

Ghost ponies have been seen on Exmoor, and moorland Red Deer disappear into the mist – when there is no mist. Supernatural tales of hares surround these mysterious creatures: witches were associated with them, and one folktale tells of an Exmoor inn keeper, Fanny Pope, believed to be a witch who could shapeshift into a hare. Hunters heard her grandson shouting, "Run Granny or they will catch you!" and then saw a hare running for its life as they gave chase. Later, back at the inn, they found Fanny out of breath and very dishevelled.

Well, legends are legends after all.

CATS

North Devon has its share of supernatural animals. The cat at Tarr Steps, and a black cat appears then vanishes again near Barnstable's civic centre. Hunting ghostly mice, perhaps?

The Exmoor Beast, however, is more intriguing. Reminiscent of Conan Doyle's canine supernatural story, *The Hound of the Baskervilles*, (set on Dartmoor, not Exmoor), the North Devon Wild Cat was mentioned in *Country Life* magazine:

> *"A dark shape some five foot long, crouched over the top of a hedge, green eyes glaring at the truck. The driver moved back up the slope to get a better look, but the animal disappeared in the shadows."*
> [Sighting of the Beast of Exmoor *Country Life* September 2002]

Is this a ghost, a roaming wild cat or the product of fanciful imagination? Mention of a Big Cat has been in circulation since the 1970s, although sightings are unlikely to be of the same animal. Reports of an elusive feline have been claimed by a variety of people, but definite proof has never been established. Witnesses talk of a large creature resembling a golden-brownish puma.

North Devon farmers frequently report sightings of large, catlike creatures. In 1983 several sheep were found dead on Exmoor with their throats ripped out, and the carcasses partially eaten. Even though a group of Royal Marines were sent for, nothing was found, but the sightings continue. And the stories continue to grow.

A ghost of a feral Big Cat? In this instance there is no supernatural element, for Kathy and I have seen it, or a descendant or similar animal. We were coming home one night in the car along the lanes when something big with what looked like a puma's tail appeared ahead. A fleeting glimpse only, for it jumped over the hedge into the fields. A year or so later Kathy saw a similar cat. She could have been seeing something supernatural, except the person in the car with her also had a clear view. A large, puma-like cat leapt over the hedge into the lane illuminated by the car's headlights as it jumped over the hedge on the other side of the lane. The next day the carcass of a partially eaten roe deer was found in a nearby field.

No ghost, but a *real* Big Cat. It definitely exists.

HORSES

The year 2023, one way or another, had been emotionally fraught for my family; a personal upheaval with everything unexpectedly thrown up in the air and landing again in a new, very different, pattern of everyday life. Soon after, we lost two horses and almost a third within six weeks of each other. The third horse, Lexie, thank goodness, recovered.

We bought Saffie (La Rafale) a year after moving to Devon. She was not an easy horse to ride, 'quirky' is an apt description, but understanding her foibles resulted in a gem of a mare.

Saffie, proud of her daughter, Phoenix (Taw River Nemberatas)

As she aged her breathing became steadily laboured, exacerbated in the spring of 2023 when the blossom was in full bloom, along with excessive humidity. One evening in June her lungs failed her. The vet made her comfortable but we had reached the last service we could do for her. She is buried in our field, but Kathy has seen her grazing contentedly several times since.

Then we lost four-year-old Franc, Saffie's son. Tests after a freak accident revealed that he had irreparable spinal damage. There was nothing we could do. Like his mum, he has been back a few times to check that all is well.

Saffie and Franc, one week old. Now together again in pastures new

Kathy Hollick competing Franc (Taw River Dracarys) in his first and last cross-country event, a few months before we lost him. Photograph: by kind permission © Rob Bayes Photography

Our Franc has come back to visit several times

DOGS

Torrington has a black dog, seen occasionally running alongside the Torrington to Bideford road before it vanishes, while not far from South Molton, a driver had to break hard when a Great Dane ran out in front of the car. With the vehicle at a halt, the dog came up to the driver's window, as if apologising for the inconvenience, then disappeared.

Rum

We lost Rum a few weeks after moving to Devon, an old boy by then, cruelly abused before we gave him a loving home. His replacement, Baz, left us in early 2024, having been with us – as a Dog's Trust Rescue – since March 2013. He had been found wandering, abandoned, in Ilfracombe. Both were loyal, loving, happy dogs, very much loved by us and very much missed. Their spirits have now moved on, but both are still very much here in our hearts and thoughts.

Our boy, Baz. Very much missed © Tony Smith

OTHER CREATURES

The most interesting animal Kathy has encountered is a very old creature in our woods. On the first sighting she described it as a Sabre-Toothed Tiger, but subsequent sightings have shown it to be a Scimitar Cat. At just under four feet in height, and slightly longer in length, bones of the Scimitar Cat have been found in Kents Cavern, South Devon, the remains dating back to about four-hundred-thousand years ago, although they roamed much of Europe from about three-million years ago until their extinction soon after the last Ice Age. Their large upper canine teeth had serrated edges, and the animal Kathy has seen had a tawny brown coat, long fore legs, muscular shoulders and a slightly sloping back, giving the impression of a powerful hunting beast. It is always in the same place and position, so, fortunately, is totally harmless.

Kathy has encountered a large, hairy brown bear in our woods near the waterfall, again initially a bit scary, but, thankfully, of no threat in today's time and place.

Our waterfall near where a brown bear lingers

CONCLUSION
A FRIENDLY GHOST IS FOR LIFE, NOT JUST FOR HALLOWE'EN.

The one certainty of life is that it ends in death. Most of us hope to reach a ripe old age before passing on with peaceful dignity and in loving, comfortable, surroundings. Sadly, and sometimes tragically, this is not always the case. People die from natural causes alone and estranged from families. Terrible accidents happen, wars take many lives, civilians and soldiers. The innocent fall victim to crime or, distressingly, those with a troubled mind take their own life.

In some cases these bewildered spirits linger for a while, puzzled as to what happened, wondering where they are and why. Encountering these troubled souls can be emotionally unsettling, and an experienced Medium will, with gentle compassion, quietly and privately assist such a spirit to peacefully move on.

Public seances, fortune tellings, or meetings held in theatres and such are, on the whole, designed for supernatural-based entertainment – and to make money. Be aware that many are nothing more than artful trickery and deception.

'Crossing a palm with silver', although nowadays it is more often a £5 or £10 note, might not bring a genuine result.

Be dubious if several leading questions have to be asked. The real McCoy will require only a bare minimum of help from you – if that. By all means enjoy the fun of the fortune teller at the local fair, but be sceptical. Many genuine Mediums will refuse financial reward when help is desperately needed.

Do ghosts exist, or are they figments of our imagination? A lack of scientific evidence to prove something does exist is not proof that it doesn't. Black Holes and the Boson Higgs Particle were nothing but conjecture until they were, eventually, proven, but those who explored their possible existence were not ridiculed. Ghosts are something that might or might not be there, so perhaps we should keep a polite, open mind? There are a lot of things that animals cannot see or hear but humans can and vice versa. Horses do not 'see' the colour orange, bats have a higher hearing frequency, owls have a different visual spectrum. Maybe, certain gifted people have an additional sensory perception?

Is there another dimension beyond those that are known? Even today the number is debatable, ranging to as many as ten and even more possibilities, while other thoughts veer to just the basic three or four: length, width and height, plus the addition of time. Do echoes of the past exist as another dimension, crumpled up alongside and within the one we presently inhabit and are familiar with?

CONCLUSION

Discovering the answer to "Do ghosts exist?" is an ongoing puzzle depending on personal belief, but in general the answer is:

"If you have not seen a ghost, then no they don't exist. If you have seen one, then, yes, they do."

Kathy Hollick

EXTRA ENCOUNTERS

Ghosts, spirits, lingering souls, they remain among us here in North Devon (and elsewhere of course) – maybe Kathy will have the occasional new or renewed encounter, but rather than having to think about occasionally updating this little book, we have opened an ongoing Blog where additional and new information can be regularly added. You will also find there, colour editions of all the photographs included within these pages.

You'll find the blog here:
https://ghostencountersofdevon.blogspot.com
Kathy and I look forward to meeting you there.

Helen:
Website: https://helenhollick.net
All Helen's books are available on Amazon:
https://viewauthor.at/HelenHollick

Kathy:
Website: https://www.white-owl.co.uk/
Facebook: Taw River Equine Events
https://www.facebook.com/groups/1491518561152309

A BONUS: TWO SHORT STORIES
BY HELEN HOLLICK

As a fiction writer, stories have always been my passion. I wrote pony stories as a thirteen-year-old, desperately wanting a pony, but we couldn't afford one so I invented my own in the form of fiction. I was always writing or reading, wrapped up in my own, contented world, and assumed that everyone was the same. I was somewhat bewildered to discover that this wasn't the case.

From pony stories I wrote fantasy and science fiction, then historical fiction and now I write several different genres, including short stories. Two I would like to share with you. *The Old House* was originally written for Street Life an anthology to raise money for *Emmaus Cornwall*, a charity for the homeless, The Bridge I wrote exclusively for this book, *Ghost Encounters*...

The Old House

They pulled the house down. My heart was pulled apart along with it.

Like me, it was old; slates were missing from the scullery roof, the thatch was worn – even the mice had abandoned that gape-holed roof, and the bats had moved out to new night skies long ago. None of the windows had ever closed properly; it wasn't a mere draught that whistled in through those ill-fitting frames, but a howling gale, even when there wasn't much wind. The chimneys smoked. In the kitchen, the slate floor was cracked and uneven, and anything made of wood was riddled with woodworm. Mould carpeted most of the walls where wallpaper had long since peeled away. Was it surprising that they pulled it all down? The house had been built when King Hal had taken Jane Seymour as his third wife, and the maid had died giving birth to his only son. *Divorced, beheaded, died. Divorced beheaded, survived.* I've always felt sorry for those poor maids – all of them. If only someone had been able to tell Henry that one of our greatest queens was his second daughter, Elizabeth I.

The house had witnessed the soldiers trooping to and fro along the valley below. Cromwell's New Model Army and King Charles' Royalists. Aye, and the old house had heard that sound, louder than the overhead boom of thunder when the gunpowder, stored in the crypt beneath the church over Torrington way, had ignited while battle between the two armies had raged through the town's narrow, cobbled streets. Many a good man, on both sides of that dreadful conflict of religious belief, had died that sad, sorry day.

The house had its memories, as do I. It was old, that house, old, like me... but to pull it down? Reduce it to nothing but a pile of dust and rubble? Inevitable, I suppose, when things get old and are no longer fit for purpose.

It had been a family house, full of love and laughter. Did they not know that old houses have a soul? That the echoes of the past are captured between the walls, are sealed beneath the roof? If they had stopped long enough to *listen* they would have heard the echoes, the laughter, the love. The cries of the newborn safely delivered from the womb, the joy of children playing on sun-baked days, or huddled around the table in the kitchen, their red hands, chilblained feet and glowing faces turned towards the great open fire, eager for Mother to stir the pot suspended over the flames and serve the bubbling broth within into earthenware dishes. To smell the mouth-watering aroma of fresh-baked bread. To smear new-churned butter and sweet, sweet honey on thick-cut slices.

Harsh words, too, oft times spoken when patience frayed. What families did not share the occasional tempest? Chores not done, bones weary from lambing or ploughing, worry gnawing at heart and mind when rain blighted crops or sickness crept nearer? Aye, angry words spoken, but usually quickly forgiven and forgotten. Although, not always. I smile at my memories. Mother would complain when the menfolk trooped into her clean kitchen with mud or cow-slurry on their boots. She appreciated the jugs of fresh milk brought in, though. We, in turn, appreciated the cream she made. The butter, the cheese...

They knocked the chimney down first. Three feet thick it was, with the old iron, bread oven nested beside the fireplace. I sat and watched them do the deed, although they had no idea I was hiding there. I kept out of sight for the house was no longer mine. All I had of the place was its history and my own, fond, memories.

Ah! They have found the shoe, and the bones of the cat. I'd always suspected they were there, buried in a cavity amongst the brickwork of that chimney, for it had, so folk tales recounted, been a tradition to ward off bad luck, witches and ghosts. Perhaps the tokens had done the trick, for the house had always held good luck. I am not sure of the significance of the shoe. Maybe the cat's bones kept mice and rats away? As for the witches, that must have worked for in all the years, I have never seen a witch squinnying around the windows or doors. Never seen a hag spying on the house from the garden, or watching from the dense canopy of the old oak tree.

That had gone as well. The Old Oak. The autumn storm had finally caused its end, blowing it down – right onto the house, which, I suppose, is why they were now demolishing it. The tree had been the final nail in the coffin – our coffin, mine and my home's. It had been a splendid great-great – oh, I do not know how many 'greats' – grandfather of an oak. Planted way, way back. No one was sure exactly when. Some said it was to mark the defeat of the Armada by Drake. A Devon man. South Devon, admitted, but North Devon, Appledore, along by the rivers Taw and Torridge, had sent ships to join the great fleet and to fight against the Spanish.

But the oak had been there before that, when Richard of the White Boar had become king. Had he murdered those nephews of his in London's Tower? Who knew the truth? Only he and their murderer I suppose. If indeed they were slain. Perhaps they'd fled in secret and lived their lives in safe contentment somewhere in exile. Here in Devon perhaps, farming the land. Or had they been homeless, like I am now?

I sit here, concealed within the dense thicket of dogwoods, rose briars and brambles. Yes, brambles; they have not been cleared for many a while, and they do infiltrate so. The people who took my house from me had done nothing with the garden, yet it had, once, been such a beautiful garden. Roses – red and pink and white all with the aroma of Heaven. Blue and purple lavender, which the honey bees and fat bumbles so loved. Peonies, foxgloves, violas... As many herbs as you could name growing in the little walled area set aside for them. Thyme, sage, marjoram, rosemary, cumin, hyssop, rue, dill... All overgrown now, and gone to seed. Swallows had nested every year in the barns, stables and dairy. Along with the housemartins, sparrows and little Jenny Wrens. They will need to find new homes now. As will I.

There, it has all gone. Nothing left of my home except an area of spoiled land, ruts and mess. My beautiful home. Gone.

The winter was cold. Frost, snow and that bitter, bitter northeast wind which blew through every nook, cranny and broken window in the barn where I took what shelter I could. I was too miserable to think of the cold, of a face frozen like the ice in the stream where the waterfall had become a sculptured cascade. It would all melt when the sun returned. If the sun returned. Sometimes, huddled, lonely and I admit, afraid, in the dark of the barn. I often wondered if the sun would ever shine again.

I managed to hide throughout the winter in that old barn. They'd left it standing, and had left the pile of old hay that had been there for years. It was musty, but served its purpose. I shared it with a hibernating dormouse, and a barn owl stared at me from its perch high among the rafters, looking down at me as the winter daylight faded into dusk. I marvelled as she spread her wings and glided, silent as a secret whisper out through the open door and was gone into the night. They used to say that the White Owl was an omen of death, the spirit of one departed. I could well believe it.

There were tawny owls too, out in the woods. A vixen barking to her mate, badgers snuffling for roots, worms and what they could find – finally finishing off what little was left of my garden! When the snow was at its thickest and heaviest, the Lords and Ladies of Exmoor came down to forage for what they could find. I heard them, but only saw one of them; a stag resplendent in his reddish-brown coat with the spread of his fourth and fifth tines forming into a fitting crown, although his noble appearance was spoiled by the ragged shedding of the velvet. I think he knew I was there, for he stood a long while, head high, as still as a carved statue. Then he moved as fast as lightning flashes, and was gone.

I slept during those long winter months, unaware of what the world was doing outside. Then, with the spring, others came. More noise, more disruption. Banging, clattering, hammering, drilling... I covered my ears and huddled deeper into the dark, concealing shadows of the woods where I now hid. I shut my ears, my eyes, my senses. Shut it all out. This was no longer my home and I cared nothing for them as they cared nothing for me.

I stayed there, safe within the new-grown bracken and uncurling, shepherd's crook-shaped ancient ferns, safe in the dappled shade of the hawthorn, beech, birch and ash. Safe, even when it all stopped and all I could hear was the sound of the leaves, dancing in the wind, and the cows in the valley below lowing at milking time. The ewes calling, anxious, to their skittering lambs, and the pheasants clucking their absurd cries of alarm. The woods were my home now, and unless – until – they found me and moved me on, here I would stay. Except, one late summer evening I did venture out, just to look. Just once, I told myself. I would look just the once to see what these new people had done to my home.

They had rebuilt it. There was a high, sturdy chimney. There was new thatch, covering arched oak beams. I peeped through a window – new slate flags on the kitchen floor, new cupboards, everything new but in the style of what I had known and loved when this had been my home.

They were a family, Father, Mother, three children – two girls and a boy. Oh, I was pleased about that, my old home needed children to fill it with love and laughter. One of them, the eldest girl by the look of her, glanced up from what she was doing and stared at me peering through the window. I willed her to not shout out, to not draw attention. I put my finger to my lips: *sssh*! Would she stay as quiet as that dormouse in the barn? As silent as that spread-winged angel-owl?

She did not shout, or scream, but smiled at me. I smiled back.

This used to be my home, I thought. *My home, where I had lived and laughed and loved*. Would this new family learn to love this new house as much as I had the old one? I turned away from the window, the sting of tears in my eyes, my heart as heavy as death. This was their home now. Not mine.

Then I heard her voice, the girl's voice, clear in my mind.

It is our home now, sir, but you are most welcome to share it.

I slipped withindoors that night. Crept, as silent as a shadow up the new-built oak staircase, watched the children as their mother snuggled them into their beds and kissed them goodnight as I had, once, kissed and cuddled my dear children.

I heard her again, the eldest girl. Heard her say, quietly, to her mother:

"Did you know, Mum, that we've got a ghost? I think he used to live here, and would like to live here again, with us in our new home."

"He will be most welcome. I suspect he's lived here a long, long time, and loves this house as much as we do."

The girl smiled at me, and I smiled back.

© Helen Hollick

The Bridge

The hour was early, at least gone two according to the clock on the church tower that cleaved to the hill above the night-quiet town. The winter weather was miserable, cold and wet with a bitter north-east wind that gnawed ravenously at exposed hands and faces. Yesterday's forecast had predicted snow. It hadn't come, but it wasn't far off if the vicious bite in the air was anything to go by. Winter? It was April already, it would be Easter next week. What was that he'd seen on Twitter? Something about statistically it was more likely to snow at Easter than at Christmas? Twitter? X? Stupid name, 'X'. What did it mean? X for unknown? X for 'marks the spot' as if the social media platform was a pirate's treasure map, the end of the quest, the end of the adventure. The X, showing where the treasure was buried. Except, he had no map, no treasure to find. He'd lost everything – not that he'd ever had much to lose in the first place.

He'd liked Twitter's Larry the Bluebird, the cheerful little fellow had conveyed what the site was all about: friendly chatter, lots of voices all merrily twittering away together like the garden birds during the dawn chorus or a sunny, spring evening. X indicated X-rated, nil, nothing tangible or something hidden, anonymous. Like in the olden days for people who couldn't write their name so had to put an X instead of a signature. A nobody. Like he was. A nothing. A waste of space nobody lingering in the shadows, unseen, unnoticed. Unwanted.

Chris turned his frayed collar higher and ducked his chin deeper into his zipped-up jacket; shoved his ungloved hands into his pockets. Ha! X or *ex*? Something that was once but wasn't now.

He shivered again. 'Nothing' did much to ease the cold seeping into and through him. 'Nothing' did much to ease the empty ache that chewed at his insides, devouring, or so it felt, his very guts. He was a failure. No denying it. His supervisor at the garage, last week, hadn't said as much, but it was there, obvious in the way he'd looked – arms folded, brows creased into a frown. Eyes with not even the slightest spark of sympathetic understanding. He'd oozed disappointment and resignation.

Chris was familiar with that look, he'd seen it all the time at school, seen it in the faces of every teacher from primary to senior school. *You're a failure, Christopher. Everything you do ends in failure. You don't try hard enough, that's your problem. I don't know why we bother with you.*

His parents had said the same. *You don't try, Chris*! The garage supervisor hadn't actually *said* those same words, but Chris had known he was thinking them. Unlike his girlfriend who *had* said exactly that.

Another X. *Ex*-girlfriend? What had she been? A friend, he supposed, not really a girlfriend, although that's how he'd thought of her. She'd been someone to talk with, laugh with. Someone to look to a brighter future with rather than endure this dismal, not-so-merry merry-go-round existence. She wasn't a girlfriend. That relationship status had only existed in his dreams, his hopes, his whimsy. She was pretty, she was nice. Obviously the 'nice' bit he'd got wrong too. Whatever she had or hadn't been, she was an ex now.

"You know your trouble, Chris?" she had said, spitefully, one scrunched fist on her hip, the Christmas lights at the shopping centre bright behind, making her curly blonde hair look like it was glowing with the circlet of an angel's halo. "Your trouble is, you don't *think*. You believe yourself to be some sort of handsome Superman – but leave nothing behind you except failed, catastrophic consequences for everyone else to clear up or sort out."

They'd been at the shopping centre together on Boxing Day because that was the only way to see her – carry her bags when she wanted to go shopping. Her parents wouldn't let him in their house, they said he was a 'bad sort'. Not that he was sure what they meant by 'bad sort'. He was polite. Most of the time. He'd never broken the law, didn't take drugs – didn't have enough guts to steal, so had no money to buy 'stuff'.

He'd always been the one to get the blame for things, though. At school it was always him who'd been ordered to stand in the corner or sent to the head for a ticking off. But he'd never *done* anything, it was always the others putting the blame on him. And he'd been too slow to realise, and too much of a nobody to defend himself against them. He'd been suspended from school when he was fifteen for a whole term. The best days of his life: no school, no bullies. But also, nothing to do, nowhere to go except hang about where no one noticed him.

"I've got you a present," he'd said to his girlfriend as he'd shyly handed her a small box wrapped in silver foil which he'd nicked from his mum's drawer in the kitchen. The girl had laughed when she'd opened it. Not a *fun* laugh, a sarcastic, mocking, laugh.

"This is a plastic engagement ring!" she'd scoffed.

"Yes," Chris had answered, smiling warmly and hopefully at her. "It's meant to be a diamond."

"But it's the sort of kiddies' rubbish you get in cheap Christmas crackers."

He managed to keep the smile. That's exactly where he'd got the ring from. A squashed cracker at Christmas dinner. Not turkey and roast spuds; Mum had forgotten to buy turkey and potatoes. Christmas dinner had been beans on toast.

The smile faded. "I can't afford anything else," he'd muttered. "One day, though, I'll get you the real thing."

"No thanks. I don't like rubbish, and anyway, what makes you think I'd marry *you*?" She'd tossed the cheap ring into a litter bin, grabbed the three shopping bags full of Primark bargains and walked off. Had tossed over her shoulder: "You're a loser, Chris. I intend to marry someone with money, someone who knows where he's going... up!"

He'd never seen her again.

The afternoon his supervisor had summoned him to his office he'd given platitudes like: *I had faith in you Christopher*, and, *I truly thought you had it in you to shine*. And as a kindly meant but hurtful barely concealed mutter: *perhaps one day you will*. He hadn't added the *but*. Although Chris knew he'd thought it. *But I doubt it*.

Was that a snowflake? Wrinkling his nose, screwing his eyes into slits to see better, Chris peered into the feeble streetlamp-lit darkness ahead. It could be snow, could be sleet.

He'd been accused of slacking, of not doing the job he was supposed to have done. But he had... he *had*! What use arguing though? The lady had brought her car back, oil dripping everywhere, even though the oil leak had been fixed the day before. The oil cap had been left off. Oil had sloshed everywhere; cleaning it up – free of charge – had been a big job. And after, Chris had been 'let go', blamed for the carelessness. He *knew* he'd put that cap back on properly, he remembered turning it tight, checking it. The supervisor hadn't believed him and the other apprentice had stood there, sniggering.

Ahead was The Bridge. It had an official name, but everyone local simply called it *The Bridge*. It spanned the broad river linking the residential side of town to the industrial estate, where offices, warehouses and extensive showrooms were filled with people by day and became a ghost town by night. Ideal for the unloved, unwanted shadow people, like Chris, to hide.

Two cars came past, their headlights dazzling him. There was hardly any traffic at this hour; sensible people were snug in their beds. Who would be stupid enough to be out in this weather, at this hour? Only fools and failures.

He'd taken refuge in a cheap café until they'd finally closed, then he'd walked to nowhere in particular, just walked. He'd given up going home a while ago. Dad was usually drunk in front of the telly, the front room stinking of stale cigarette smoke and booze. Mum would come home, tiddly, from Bingo. They might not have noticed him sneak up to his cold box-bedroom at the back of the unkempt house, but it had been a risk he'd been unwilling to take. There would have been a row when they discovered he'd lost his job. His meagre wage bought Dad's drink and fags and Mum's Bingo. As for the rent or food... He'd not gone home. There'd been no point.

Several of the lights further across the bridge, towards the middle, were not lit, they'd been smashed months ago by youths out for vandalism fun and the council had not considered replacing them to be a priority. Youths often messed about on the bridge, showing off, smoking fags or pot. A few months back, a girl had been gang raped where the lack of light plunged the bridge into semi-dark, deep shadow. No one had helped her, despite her terrified, pleading, screams and the gangs' cackling, excited, laughter.

After, they'd left her, part naked, battered, bruised, bleeding and ashamed. Hurting, desperate, she'd climbed onto the railings and thrown herself off into the river. Her body had been found the next day. No one had been caught or punished, not even DNA evidence had been of any use. General opinion was that the police hadn't bothered collecting any anyway. Which wasn't true, but social media rarely broadcast the truth.

Chris hunched his shoulders, burrowed his hands deeper, tucked his chin tighter and walked along the narrow pavement onto The Bridge. He didn't like this bridge, it always had a forlorn air about it. Even on the sunniest days it seemed to be wreathed in an invisible fug of despair. That girl had not been the first to jump off into the black, cold, uncaring water below. There had been others, men, women, girls, boys. The youngest had been ten, the eldest seventy. All with one thing in common. They'd abandoned hope.

There were others, too. Rumour had it that there were bodies buried within the sturdy supporting pillars. Bodies that had been encased – alive maybe – in the concrete as it had been poured in. The bodies of snitches, betrayers, traitors or those unfortunates who'd not had the money to pay what they owed to the crooks and the gangs. The bodies of doomed failures.

Chris shuddered; not just from the cold.

Glancing sideways to avoid the full glare of another passing car's full beam headlights, he could see the black swirl of the river through the vertical struts of the metal railings. Cold, dark and deep. The tide was in at full, high tide, the current wallowing at slack water. Soon it would turn, become the ebb and sweep any flotsam and jetsam out to the estuary and beyond to the open sea a few miles away. When it was fully out, the depth dropped by about fifteen feet, the banks being exposed as swathes of smelly, muddy sand, decorated here and there with old bikes, rusting supermarket trollies, plastic bottles, discarded tins, used condoms, broken hypodermic needles and such. Even the most eager of detectorists had given up searching those mudflats for possible treasure. They were more likely to come away with some transmissible disease or a rat bite.

Perhaps because of the swirling black water below the bridge, or the falling sleet – sleet, still, not snow – it looked like some of the shadows ahead were moving. Ghouls and ghosties, or yobbos out for a lark? At this point, Chris didn't care. If they were troublemakers intent on beating him up, so what? It wouldn't matter.

He was near the middle now, one of the street lights on the

opposite side of the road hadn't been completely broken, but it was flickering erratically in an apparent last-ditch death agony. It tossed out enough scattered light for Chris to make more sense of one of the lingering shadows. A girl? It looked like a girl, although he couldn't be certain. He squinted, part shielded his eyes with one hand. Yes! A girl had climbed over the railings, was sitting on the top rail, her legs dangling on the far side, her bare hands gripping the cold steel. Her shoulders were hunched, her head drooped, long, straggly, fair hair hiding her face, chin on her chest.

What should he do? What *could* he do? This was something he had not expected, not on this cold, bleak night when he'd wanted to be alone. Should he simply walk past? Pretend he hadn't noticed her? He couldn't cross over to the other side of the road – there was no footpath on that side, he was likely to get hit by a car. Hah! That would be ironic! All his problems solved by a driver who'd not seen him walking, hunched in the dark shadows. But that wouldn't be fair on an innocent driver, would it? There'd be police and enquiries. If the driver had been drinking he – maybe she – would lose his or her licence, and that would all be Chris's fault too.

Perhaps he should stop? Talk to her? What for? Why? He'd probably only make the situation worse.

She made no sign that she'd seen or heard him as he slunk past.

Walk, don't run, Chris thought to himself, but a yard beyond, he increased his pace. Ten yards and he was jogging. Another twenty-five and he'd be off the bridge, safe on the other side. He stopped. And that too, would be a failure, wouldn't it?

He turned round, walked back to the girl, stopped two yards away from her and taking his hands from his pockets, rested his arms on the railings to stare down into the black, sinister depth of the tidal river. He tucked each hand into each sleeve to keep his fingers at least a little warm. Well, less cold.

"It's deep here," he said. "They reckon about thirty feet at high tide. Soft landing if you get to the bottom without breaking your neck because it's all mud, the riverbed." He peered further over. "It's a long way down. A long way to jump." He felt in his pocket, found his house front door key. Huh, he'd not be needing *that* again. He deliberately dropped it into the water. It was too dark to see, soon lost sight of it, and the gushing river too noisy to hear any faint 'plop'. He shoved his hand back into his sleeve. "Mind, there are a couple of boulders somewhere near here. That great flood a few years back brought them down from upriver. No one's cared to try to move them. The boulders don't bother the canoes, kayaks or sailing dinghies, all shallow on the draught, you see. Not so good for jumpers – people who jump from here, that is, not woolly sweaters. Jumpers don't know where the boulders are. Hit one of them head on..." He withdrew one hand and smacked it on the top of the railing, sending the metal humming and juddering for most of its length. He noticed her grip tighten. "Smack!" he cried. "Makes rather a mess. Mind, the water washes the blood away, and it's a quicker end than drowning, I suppose."

The girl made no answer, no movement beyond that tightened grip. She sat there, as still as a statue, hunched, forlorn, not really hearing this intruder but not having the inclination to tell him to leave her alone, to piss off.

"I wonder what's better?" He frowned, considering; "Smashing your head open for a quick ending, or being tossed about in that current, slowly drowning as your body tries to breathe but fills your lungs with water instead of air? Once you're in it's usually the end. That water's like ice – freezing, even in the summer. No one can get to help you quick enough, you see. 'Specially at night when there's no one around to see you jump."

Chris slid his hand back into his sleeve. That definitely was a snowflake. Another, then another fell. *How many thousands of snowflakes does it take to make a blizzard?* he wondered.

"I used to surf as a kid," he said, "nothing fancy, I was in a kid's club. Learnt a lot, enjoyed it. I used to swim in this river, too, oh, years ago now, well before..." he shrugged. "Well before Nan died when I was fifteen. Further along though, upriver, near one of the villages where she lived. I miss Nan. She looked out for me." He was silent a moment, swallowing down sad memories. He had been a good, confident swimmer, aware of how dangerous strong currents could be. "The water's only a few feet deep or so upriver – in non-flood seasons. Winter, or when it hardly stops raining, you're talking twice that. Current's strong too, like it is here so close to the estuary. Rip tides, you see, strong currents running out to sea. They can drag people away from the shallows and out to deep water, flowing at one to two miles an hour, but can reach four or five – faster than an Olympic swimmer. You mustn't underestimate the power of water. You get rip tides down there, around the piers of this bridge. You shouldn't call them rip *tides*, though everyone does. Properly, they're rip *currents*. Only an idiot would swim near those currents." Chris stopped talking. Only an idiot. He'd been an idiot, a prize idiot, more than once. Now, here he was being, talking like, an idiot again.

"It's a bit final, isn't it? Jumping from this bridge. The sort of thing that losers and failures do. A last act of defiance, maybe? Something to show that a decision made can be a decision accomplished?"

He looked at the girl. He still couldn't see her face. All he could see was the tip of her nose and the pointy bit of her chin protruding from that curtain of hair. Maybe she was really pretty, maybe the opposite, disfigured or ugly? Who cared? It wasn't what you *looked* like, it was how you were *inside that mattered. What makes you tick as a person. Kindness is better than cleverness.* That's what Nan had always told him. *People respect kindness, get bored with arrogant cleverness. You don't need to be clever to be kind.*

"I'm Chris," he said, "and I mess up everything I do. Hopeless at school. Never could grasp what them squiggly things on paper were meant to be. Took me years to learn to read. Still not very good at it, though Nan took the time, and patience, to teach me. It would've helped if the words had kept still, but they move about the page like a herd of ants scurrying about. Is ants a herd? That doesn't sound right. Flock? Troop? March? Army? Ah, perhaps it's army. Anyway, I'm dyslexic. Doesn't make much difference to me, I get by, but I get muddled. Make a mess of things. Others make fun of me, call me thicko and stupid. It's always been me who gets into trouble, never them. It was OK when I was with Nan, she used to stick up for me. Mum and Dad don't care. No one cares. Even I don't care. Not now, anyway."

He looked again, sideways, at her. She was shivering, he could see that. She was wearing a short leather jacket – a nice leather jacket – jeans, and walking boots. They'd help weigh her down if she jumped. When she jumped.

"I don't do so bad on my mobile phone," Chris said, a small smile playing on his mouth as he pulled his phone from his pocket and played, one-handed with a few buttons. "It's only a cheap phone, not one of these fancy things. I can't afford those." The pale light from the phone illuminated his face. A good, firm face that had sagged through the burden of hopeless despair. "Text on a screen doesn't move about, see? And text spelling isn't as fussy as proper spelling, so I get by. I thought I was getting by at the garage as a mechanic, but I got sacked a couple of days ago for something I didn't do... I mean I *did* do it, but they said I didn't." He sighed. "That doesn't make sense, does it? They said I hadn't put the oil cap back on, but I had. One of the others must have taken it off again and I got the blame. So now I'm out of work, I don't want to go home, and I don't know what to do."

That was a lie. He knew perfectly well what he was going to do.

Chris sighed again, and glanced down at the water through the swirl of wind-skittering snowflakes that were falling heaver now. He heaved himself up and sat, just like the girl, on the top rail, legs dangling, hands gripping, the rail cold on his bum and thighs through the thin material of his jeans.

"You going to jump then?" he asked. "I rather hope you're not, because, you see, if you do, I'll be obliged to jump in and rescue you. And then there's those boulders. I'd forgotten about those until I saw you sitting here. Jumping into the river could be quick and fairly painless in this cold, but if you hit those boulders, it might be different. Head first you'll be OK. Smash... and you're dead. But what if you get a broken leg, or hip or back or arm? Gawd, that'll hurt a bit, won't it?" Chris stared down at the ripples and rivulets of water, focused on where it slopped and splashed against the bridge supports. Here and there, where the current swirled towards the centre of the river, sparkles of white foam glittered and gleamed in the feeble reflection from the few working streetlights. "Do sea horses turn into river horses once they've breached the estuary?" he wondered aloud. "Nan read me stories from books when she was alive. Super books, *Treasure Island*, *The BFG*, *Matilda*, *Harry Potter* – all of them. I've never forgotten a single one of the books she read to me. One was *The Little White Horse*. It was a bit girly, but I loved the thought of those white horses rushing in with the tide and turning into unicorns as soon as their little sea hooves touched the shore."

He paused, turned his head to see if she was laughing at him for being so foolish. "I like stories like those. Made up stuff. It's better than this shit reality."

She wasn't laughing; he wasn't sure that she was even listening. Was he wasting his breath? What more could he say? Talk about? "I didn't like working at the garage, the smell of oil made me gag. I'd rather do something I was good at, but I'm not good at anything."

Except swimming and caring about people. The words slid into his head. "Except swimming. I wonder if the local pool needs lifeguards? You don't need to be able to read well to be a lifeguard, do you?" His following sigh was louder than any previous one. "Look, I don't want to seem selfish, or callous or anything, but do you think you could get down? Move to somewhere else? I came here to think, to be on my own, and to..." He stopped. He *was* being selfish and callous.

A car had pulled up at the end of the bridge, its headlights dimmed. Two uniformed men had got out, were walking, slowly and quietly. Policemen.

"Hello," the taller of the coppers said in a friendly voice as he stopped walking and stood three yards away. "Not quite the best place to sit and admire the view, eh?" he added.

"Bit cold," said the other, shorter, more rotund officer. "And it's snowing heavier. Snow at Easter? Who'd have thought it? A nice warm all-night café with a mug of tea and a bacon butty sounds more appealing to me, rather than being out here, looking at the river."

"How about you get down and come with us for that cuppa?" the taller one suggested. "We're due for a break; be nice to have some young company to chat to."

Chris stared at them. He'd always got on with coppers, but then all the times he'd messed up he'd never done anything that went against the law. "I wanted to be a policeman when I was a kid," he said, "but the teachers all said I was too stupid because of my dyslexia."

"Dyslexia doesn't mean you can't try for things you want to do," the short policeman said.

"I'd still like to be a policeman," Chris answered. "Help people when they're in trouble."

"We're always needing bright youngsters to join us. Why not apply?" said the tall one. "You've nothing to lose, and you can get help where and when you need it. My cousin's dyslexic, and he's in C.I.D."

"Can't do that from up there though, mate," said the short man. "Why not hop down and come for that cup of tea? We can talk about the possibilities of becoming a copper, or some alternatives, in the warm and dry."

Chris shrugged. He'd had every intention of ending it all, that's why he was on The Bridge. High Tide, less likelihood of hitting those boulders, although the cold would kill him as effectively. The girl had put paid to that idea. If he hadn't stopped to talk to her, talk *her* out of jumping, he'd be in the river and dead by now. A body, a corpse, floating down there with the now ebbing tide.

Looking firmly eye to eye at the taller of the two policemen, he climbed back over the railings, found, as his feet touched the pavement, that his legs were shaking – and not just from the cold. He had to see to the girl. If he had to fail at his own suicide, then by heck, he'd make sure that she failed as well!

He turned round, one hand on the railing to steady his balance. There was no girl. Surely these policemen had seen her? Had she jumped? Why hadn't they made a grab for her? But there'd been no splash?

"There was a girl?" he said, puzzled, pointing at where she'd sat, his teeth chattering. "She was here, talking to me, or rather I was talking to her. She was going to jump, I, I stopped her, and texted 999 without her noticing."

The two policemen exchanged glances. There'd been no girl, only this desperate lad who'd made a desperate cry for help. With a silent nod they agreed to say nothing; who knew what went through a person's mind when they were on the brink of ending it all?

As Chris got into the back of the police car and they drove off the bridge, he was certain that he saw a girl standing there on the embankment, her hand raised in a friendly gesture, a sort of acknowledging salute. There were others gathered behind her, faint, misty shadow-shapes, all of them smiling, waving at him. Men, women, girls, boys. An old man, a young boy. But it was only the girl that he could see clearly.

She was smiling at him and she nodded, just the once.

You're no failure, Chris, you're a kind, generous young man, who will, one day, make a brilliant policeman.

He heard the words in his head, shuffled round, looked out of the car's rear window. There was no one there. No shadow-shapes, only the night-deserted bridge and the falling snow.

© *Helen Hollick*

This story is dedicated to The Samaritans, who keep a watchful eye on The Bridge.

ACKNOWLEDGEMENTS

Thank you to several Facebook groups, especially the helpful people from various North Devon towns and villages who recounted their experiences: Levi, Rachel, Dorothy, Sam, Ashley and Cheryl, George, Sally, Sarah and Marcus. [Surnames withheld.]

In particular, thank you to Vara Hrolfswiffe, Robert and Adrienne Hesketh and to Steve and Hazel Bowles and their staff at The Exeter Inn. Steve Anscombe, the former landlord at The Portsmouth Arms, Robert and the staff at The Grove, Simon Wyburn from The Staghunters Inn and former Chittlehamholt resident, Diane Lang.

To Mal for the map, Connie, Annie Whitehead, Jo, Elizabeth St.John, and Cathy Helms for their assistance in various production and publication ways. For postcards and photographs, thank you to author Richard Lethbridge, Robert Jeffries, Alison and Paul Sopp, AB, Simon Murgatroyd, Tony Smith and Robin Jacob.

Especially, my gratitude to historical artist Chris Collingwood for permission to use his superb artwork. http://www.collingwoodhistoricart.com and finally, to all the kind people who requested to remain anonymous – *thank you*.

If you have enjoyed this book, please do leave a review online. Kathy and I would be delighted to hear of any encounters with friendly spirits in the North Devon area, there must be many experiences which have not, yet, been shared. Feel free to email us via author@helenhollick.net

And if you have the honour of meeting someone from the past keep calm, smile and simply say a friendly, "Hello."

Sunrise, shadows and the presence of the past

BEFORE YOU GO

How To Say 'Thank you' to your favourite authors:
Leave a review on Amazon
https://mybook.to/GhostEncounters
http://viewauthor.at/HelenHollick
'Like' and 'follow' where you can.
Subscribe to a newsletter.
Give your favourite books as presents.
Spread the word!

FURTHER READING

FURTHER PRAISE FOR HELEN HOLLICK'S NOVELS

"Helen Hollick has it all! She tells a great story, gets her history right, and writes consistently readable books" Bernard Cornwell

"A novel of enormous emotional power" Elizabeth Chadwick

"In the sexiest pirate contest, Cpt Jesamiah Acorne gives Jack Sparrow a run for his money!" Sharon K. Penman

"Thanks to Hollick's masterful storytelling Harold's nobility and heroism enthral to the point of engendering hope for a different ending to the famous battle of 1066" Publisher's Weekly

"If only all historical fiction could be this good" Historical Novel Association Reviews

"Most impressive" The Lady

FURTHER READING

"Helen Hollick's series about piratical hero Jesamiah Acorne and his mystical wife Tiola Oldstagh provides a real comfort read that seamlessly blends history, fantasy, and romance with plenty of action and suspense while also further developing the characters with every new book."

"Loved this book as I have all the previous ones. Good story, excellent characters, well written with just enough descriptive detail of shipboard life and ways."

"I completely gobbled this one up! Captain Jesamiah Acorne has become a bit of an addiction for me."

"I really love this series from Helen Hollick. As usual she is very meticulous with historical facts and as usual you won't be able to put it down."

Also By Helen Hollick

The Pendragon's Banner Trilogy
The Kingmaking: Book One
Pendragon's Banner: Book Two
Shadow of the King: Book Three

The Saxon 1066 Series
A Hollow Crown (UK edition title)
The Forever Queen (US edition title. USA Today bestseller)

Harold the King (UK edition title)
I Am The Chosen King (US edition title)

1066 Turned Upside Down (alternative short stories by various authors)

The Sea Witch Voyages of the pirate, Captain Jesamiah Acorne
Sea Witch: The first voyage
Pirate Code: The second voyage
Bring It Close: The third voyage
Ripples In The Sand: The fourth voyage
On The Account: The fifth voyage
Gallows Wake: The sixth voyage
To follow
Jamaica Gold, The seventh voyage
When The Mermaid Sings: *a novella prequel.*

The Jan Christopher Cosy Mystery Series: Set in the 1970s
A Mirror Murder
A Mystery of Murder
A Mistake of Murder
A Meadow Murder
A Memory of Murder
(more titles to follow!)

Short stories by various authors, including contributions by Helen Hollick
Betrayal
Historical Stories of Exile

Non-fiction
Pirates: Truth and Tales
Life of a Smuggler: In Fact and Fiction

www.ingramcontent.com/pod-product-compliance
Lightning Source LLC
Chambersburg PA
CBHW030437010526
44118CB00011B/676